S0-CFB-304

CONTENTS

Associate in management (AIM). Associate in risk management (ARM). Associate in underwriting (AU). Associate in loss control management (ALCM). Associate in premium auditing (APA). Associate in research and planning (ARP). Associate in insurance accounting and finance (AIAF). The chartered life underwriter (CLU) designation.

Attorneys. Accountants. Human resources personnel. Public relations staff. Nursing and health personnel.

ABOUT THE AUTHOR

Born in Chicago, Illinois, Robert M. Schrayer attended Kenwood Grammar School, the University of Chicago Lab School, and Harvard High School before matriculating to the University of Michigan at Ann Arbor, where he received a Bachelor of Arts Degree in philosophy in 1954.

Following his graduation from the University of Michigan, he entered the insurance industry as an employee of Associated Agencies, Inc. in Chicago. He later attended the Insurance Company of North America's School for Agents, in Pennsylvania, in order to acquire specified insurance skills. Through the years, he assumed invaluable experience in the field and eventually became vice president and part owner of the insurance agency.

In 1971 Mr. Schrayer left Associated Agencies, Inc. to form his own insurance agency, Robert M. Schrayer Company. In 1986 his company purchased The Associated Agencies, Inc. and assumed operations under the banner of Associated Agencies, Inc. As of this writing, Associated Agencies, Inc. is the fourth largest insurance agency in metropolitan Chicago.

This edition was revised by Mark Rowh, a professional career book author and Director of Institutional Advancement at New River Community College in Dublin, Virginia.

FOREWORD

Although nearly 2,860,000 people in the United States are employed in the insurance business, it is likely that only a few of them actually planned to have a career in insurance. People often decide early to become a doctor, a lawyer, a dentist, a minister, a professional athlete, to go into law enforcement, or to become a firefighter, but they rarely say at age ten—"I want to be an insurance agent when I grow up."

One reason for the small number of people who make insurance an early career choice is lack of understanding of what people in insurance do, how insurance operates, and the great value insurance provides to the country's—and the world's—economy.

It is quite easy to understand, at least in general terms, what a doctor, lawyer, or police officer does, but what does an actuary do? What is a claim representative's workday like? What training do you have to have to be an insurance underwriter?

Insurance, for the most part, operates behind the scenes in every aspect of our personal and business lives. Almost everyone has homeowners' or renters' insurance to protect against loss in case of fire, robbery, or other peril such as lightning or windstorm. In most states, in order to drive a car legally, we must have liability insurance to protect others against any loss in the case of an accident in which we might be involved. We rely on health insurance to help pay for doctor appointments and other medical care. We have life insurance to protect the family in case of premature death of a wage earner. Most major economic undertakings, like building a shopping mall, transporting goods to market, or launching a new medication for heart disease, would not take place without the backing of insurance.

Insurance, then, is an integral part of all our lives. But the work involved in selling, underwriting, and administering insurance is not well understood by the general public. The insurance business has many rewarding career opportunities for people with all types of skills—interpersonal, math, organizational, technological, and business—skills required by a business that is growing and flourishing in today's robust economy.

Most people you meet who are employed in the insurance business would probably say, "I never thought I'd work in insurance. I got into it serendipitously, but I'm proud of what I do. It's challenging and rewarding, and I work with fine people."

Give some serious thought to pursuing a career in insurance. It offers great diversity, opportunity for growth in a large and challenging business, and a chance to participate in a profession that underlies the personal, financial, and economic well being of most families and businesses in the United States and throughout the world.

Terrie Edward Troxel, Ph.D., CPCU, CLU
President and Chief Executive Officer
American Institute for CPCU
Insurance Institute of America

ACKNOWLEDGMENTS

The author wishes to express his gratitude to John and Beth Tomkiw for all their research and assistance in assembling this book. Their perseverance and dedication were greatly appreciated.

In addition, the author would like to thank Dick Spencer of the Independent Insurance Agents of Illinois for his timely assistance with research.

Thanks also are extended to the employees and staff of Associated Agencies, Inc. in Chicago for their suggestions and recommendations regarding this book's content.

INTRODUCTION

What images pop into your mind when someone suggests that you consider a career in insurance? Toting a briefcase from house to house, trying to sell life insurance policies to your friends? Sitting in an office with only a calculator and a telephone for company? Think again—and try these images on for size.

How would you like to travel to exotic locations in Asia and Europe to help an international business client coordinate insurance coverage for a variety of locations? Or work in the field after a tornado or hurricane strikes to help people rebuild their lives? How about visiting factories, shop floors, and businesses to design programs that prevent workers from getting hurt? Or, if you like puzzles, you could piece together information culled from dozens of sources to determine the best way to protect a customer.

Given the dynamics of today's insurance marketplace, a career in insurance is just as likely to put you into any one of these scenarios instead of just behind a desk. Of course, you can still sell auto and life insurance to your friends and neighbors. But there's a lot more to it than that. If you're working with corporate insurance buyers, your customers could include not only international Fortune 500 companies, but baseball teams, movie studios, even entire cities and states. An insurance transaction can involve a couple of hundred dollars for a basic car insurance policy or a complex, multimillion-dollar deal involving players in locations around the world and a basketful of exotic risks.

The fact is, some of the hottest jobs in finance aren't on Wall Street at all—they're in insurance. This is a trillion-dollar business that employs more than 2.5 million people in the country alone. And, as the U.S. population grows older and more educated through the next century, experts predict that the need for insurance professionals will grow exponentially. Even the average life-and-auto insurance agent is expected to provide a wide variety of financial services and to act as a consultant to his or her personal lines customers.

No matter what your work style is, chances are there's an insurance career that will fit you like a tailor-made suit. If you're the analytical type, you might consider being an *actuary,* predicting the risk in just about anything insurable from life expectancy to the liklihood of having a car accident. *Agents* and *brokers* are consultants, advising people and businesses on the best way to protect themselves against the unforseen. *Claims adjusters* negotiate insurance claims with people and businesses after a loss—from a crumpled fender to a home blown away by a hurricane. *Risk managers* are insurance specialists working for a company and finding unique ways for that business to avoid exposure. And *underwriters* crunch the numbers to put the whole deal together, xii

Opportunities in Insurance Careers

choosing the right types of insurance with the right limits for their clients.

All of this is very different from the guy with the brief-case pitching life insurance—but in another way, it is very much the same. In spite of the job description, every career in insurance shares one common denominator: workers in this field are all dedicated to helping people and businesses protect themselves against loss. Insurance is something that everybody needs, but it takes a special type of person to understand and master the nuances involved in this deceptively simple business.

If you're considering a career in insurance, this book will provide you with some of the basics on how and where to get started. And if you never thought you'd be caught dead in insurance, it will give you a look behind the stereotypes. You might be surprised at what you find.

Ken Crerar, President
The Council of Insurance Agents and Broker

CHAPTER 1

INSURANCE: A SOLID INDUSTRY

We live in a time of great change. But one thing that is not expected to diminish is the need for insurance. In fact, with technology racing to the forefront of our society's imagination, there will be an even greater need for insurance in the future. With more people and possessions to insure as the future unfolds, the insurance industry can provide a stable career path for those who choose to work in the field.

Just what exactly is insurance? In strictest terms, insurance is defined as a financial arrangement that redistributes the costs of unexpected losses, as well as a contractual agreement in which one party agrees to compensate another party for losses. On the surface, the definition of insurance seems simple enough: someone pays another person or company a predescribed sum in order to ensure payment against certain damages, conditions, or losses.

Still, insurance is not quite so simple. The very nature of insurance is regulated—by society and governments—and the concept of insurance itself is steeped in complexities. To fully understand the insurance industry, you will want a better understanding of the very roots of insurance—its history.

HISTORY OF INSURANCE

It may surprise you to know that insurance methods have existed in some form or another for thousands of years. Before the development of modern insurance methods, insurance of another sort took place.

Thousands of years ago, when primitive people first formed social groups, a loose concept of community was formed, and with it came ideas of insurance. Anthropological data reveal that the hunters of these groups hunted together to ensure the safety of individuals. When prey was killed, the meat was shared among all members of the group, regardless of who actually captured and killed the prey. In a way, this sharing was the first form of risk spreading—ensuring the group's survival.

Much later in history, systemized insurance methods were created to ensure the livelihoods of a community's citizens.

About 4000 B.C., ingenious Chinese merchants applied the principle of risk-spreading to cargo transportation by water. During this period in history, naval methods were crude, and many ships capsized on rough waters. To maximize safety, fleets of ships traveling from one harbor to the next often split their cargoes between ships. If one merchant's ship capsized, only a portion of that merchant's goods was lost at sea. The remaining portions were safe aboard the other vessels in the loosely collected fleet.

Official recognition by legal authorities of the need for insurance occurred in 2500 B.C., when Babylonian King Hammurabi proclaimed there was a need to protect traveling merchants. At the time, Babylon was an acknowledged world leader in commerce, but thieves had taken to robbing caravans along well-traveled routes. A law passed down by Hammurabi provided that a trader would not have to repay a moneylender any monies borrowed to pay for goods in transit if those goods were lost to theft.

This law, in effect, transferred the risk from the borrower to the moneylender. In turn, the moneylender, to protect the investment, often provided patrols to accompany caravans and even discouraged others from raiding the caravans. The moneylenders further protected profitability by establishing an interest rate for the monies borrowed out. The interest was increased in direct proportion to the amount of hazard—or risk—involved in a certain trip. Thus, the first premiums, based on risk, were established.

The principle of general average—the spreading of risk to all parties concerned—was firmly established in the Middle Ages, when one merchant's cargo on a ship might be discarded to prevent a ship that was taking on water from sinking. This lightening of the load thus protected the greater investment of all the merchants' cargoes aboard the ship. In return, each merchant would pay a portion of the costs to replace the cargo that was tossed overboard—financially spreading the risks involved and establishing the first method of claims settlement.

In England during the 1600s, great progress was made in moving insurance toward modern-day reality. It was then that Edward Lloyd set up shop in London, offering sailors a respite from the travels of the sea. At Lloyd's establishment, sea captains, merchants, and traders drank tea, ate, bartered seagoing deals, and discussed insurance against financial losses. Soon it became customary for seafarers to go to Lloyd's to arrange insurance for their ships. Thus began Lloyd's of London, perhaps the most famous insurance organization in the world today.

As America grew, municipalities realized a growing need for insurance. Such disasters as the San Francisco Earthquake of 1906 (which caused $350 million in damages) and the Great Chicago Fire in 1871 (which caused $168 million in destruction) solidified the thought that formal insurance organizations were needed for towns and private citizens, as well as businesses, which were the primary users of insurance.

HOW INSURANCE SYSTEMS WORK

Insurance systems accomplish their goals by redistributing the cost of losses incurred by claims settlement. They do this through the collection of premiums (payments) from every participant in the system. In exchange for the premium, the insured (the policyholder) is promised by the insurance provider to be compensated for a loss. Because only a small percentage of those insured suffer losses, the system can redistribute the cost of losses to all members of the system.

Since risks are involved, individuals sponsored by the insurance provider calculate the risks for each policyholder and create a scale of premiums. Therefore, if a policyholder is found to have a greater risk than another policyholder in the system, higher premiums are sought. This balances the system by creating fairness for other participants who are not considered such high risks.

Beyond benefiting businesses and individuals, insurance systems benefit society. To begin with, insurance provides stability for families. By easing the hardships suffered by loss, insurance creates a more harmonious setting for families to thrive in. For instance, repairs to a burned-out home, which are initiated by a monetary settlement for the loss, allow a family to stay in the community.

Insurance is also useful to business, another integral sector of society. Insurance aids the planning process of business, since the planner would know that a property loss will not mean financial ruin. Thus, the business operator could invest more into her or his business to make it thrive, creating more revenue for the society's economy through construction and the expansion of needs.

Insurance also eases credit transactions, because lenders are more likely to provide funds if they know a debtor's death will not make collection of monies owed impossible. Lenders would also be more apt to make property loans knowing that a disaster could not destroy the financial security upon which their loan is based.

Insurance systems play an important role in creating a fair business system by abolishing the notion of monopolies. Without an insurance system, only the largest companies could survive a disaster or loss. Smaller companies would not have the income to survive fire damage to a shop, for example. However, insurance systems provide assurances that damages could be repaired and losses provided for, thus supporting a free enterprise system where even the smallest business is able to maintain a spot in the marketplace.

Most important, insurance systems bolster the economy by reinvesting the collected premiums into businesses and ventures. They in turn invest in the economy through purchases of materials and services in order to maintain their businesses.

Because society and the economy are so reliant on insurance systems, certain steps have been taken by the government to ensure that insurance systems remain solvent and just. The insurance industry itself is heavily regulated by local and federal government, with regulations enacted for every aspect of insurance business. Similarly, the insurance industry polices itself through the licensing and certification of its professionals. Later chapters in this book discuss the regulation of the insurance industry and the certification of professionals within the industry.

Insurance Industry Operators

There are two basic categories of operators in the insurance industry: the insurance company and the insurance agency.

Most frequently, the term *insurance company* refers to the insurance business that raises money by investing the premiums obtained from consumers to pay losses of other insured consumers. These consumers, the policyholders, respond directly to the company with their premium commitments, entrusting the company with their security against loss. The company, in turn, hires people to make sure the company's investments make money for the company, maintaining a surplus of capital (money). Previous examples of the insurance system's role in society were based on the workings of an insurance company.

An *insurance agency,* on the other hand, acts as a link between the insurance company and the consumer. The agency seeks out the most advantageous situation for a prospective client, working with insurance companies to find the best insurance package. Once the insurance agency has successfully linked the consumer with the best company for services, the agency receives a commission from the premium the company receives. Thus, the employee of the agency acts as the company's representative in the transaction.

Some companies employ their own agents or solicitors, who solicit customers only for that specific company. Within the insurance agency realm, however, agents may service many different companies. Thus, the agency not only represents the consumer, but the companies as well.

Originally, the term *agent* referred to a person who represented an insurance company, while *brokers* represented consumers, placing business with the companies on the consumer's behalf. In recent years, however, the line between the agent and the broker has blurred, creating a combination of the two—a person representing the consumer and the company. For the purposes of this book, brokers and agents shall be considered synonymous and shall simply be called agents.

An agency's responsibility (and the agent's, for that matter) lies in analyzing the risks that a consumer has. The agency calculates every possible loss that a particular consumer could suffer that might be protected by insurance. Once the agency understands the possibilities for potential loss, an agent then analyzes the ways in which that particular loss could be underwritten by an insurance company at a favorable premium to the consumer. (Underwriting, as applied to insurance, is defined as properly selecting insureds and charging them a rate that fairly reflects the costs and risks of providing insurance protection. Professionals who provide this service are called underwriters.)

After assembling these facts, the agency then approaches insurance companies, asking them to quote a premium they would charge to cover the specifications designed by the agent from the analysis of the consumer's risks. Once the agency has obtained a set of quotations, its task lies in analyzing the quotes to determine which insurance company would best protect the assets of the consumer. At this point, the agency also determines the cost effectiveness of the coverage, seeking for the consumer the most comprehensive coverage at the lowest cost.

If a consumer decides on purchasing an insurance company's policy, the agent who worked with the consumer then services the consumer, or account, throughout the policy period. He or she becomes, in effect, the insurance company's representative for the account or the agent for the customer.

While insurance agencies are defined by their abilities, insurance companies can also be described by the way they are classified and organized.

A particular insurance company carries one of three classifications: *domestic company, foreign company,* or *alien company.* A domestic company is one that is incorporated within a state where it does business. For example, a company incorporated in California is considered domestic by the state of California. For this reason, a company can be domestic in only one state.

By the same token, a foreign company is an insurance company incorporated in another state within the United States. For example, an insurance company incorporated in Michigan is a foreign company to the state of California.

On the other hand, an alien company is an insurance company that is incorporated in another country. For example, an insurance company incorporated in Mexico is alien to any state within the United States.

Insurance companies are also defined by how they are organized. Companies can be organized as one of four types: *stock companies, mutual companies, Lloyd's organizations,* and *reciprocal companies.* Each of these types will be discussed separately.

A stock insurance company is a company in which the initial capital investment is made by subscribers of stock.

Business then is conducted by a board of directors elected by the subscribers, or stockholders. Additionally, the distribution of earnings or profits is determined by the elected board of directors. In essence, a stock insurance company is one where stockholders contribute all the capital, pay all the losses, and reap all the profits.

A mutual insurance company is quite the opposite. While the insurance policies offered by a stock insurance company and a mutual insurance company might be similar, there are subtle differences. Members, or insureds, of a mutual insurance company have a dual relationship—they are both the insurer and the insured. They contribute to the payment of losses and are entitled to have payments made in case of a loss. In addition, they are entitled proportionately to the profits of the company.

The policyholders of a mutual insurance company have rights similar to those of stock insurance companies in that they elect company directors who, in turn, hire company officers. Company officers then hire employees who run the company.

Mutual insurance companies can issue policies that are participatory—the policyholder participates in the earnings of the company and receives dividends. These dividends are usually reflected in some sort of rate adjustment.

A Lloyd's insurance company differs from both stock insurance companies and mutual insurance companies in that each member of a Lloyd's organization is an individual insurer. In essence, each member has her or his own capital riding on a predescribed risk. A Lloyd's organization is often called an insurance pool.

The fourth type of insurance organization is the reciprocal company. In this system, several individuals may underwrite each other's risks separately. Although this type of company seems similar to the Lloyd's organization, there is one major difference: within a Lloyd's organization, all underwriting members are insurers, but not all members are insureds.

TYPES OF INSURANCE

Beyond the differences in organization, companies can be categorized by the types of insurance they provide. The broadest categories of insurance coverage are *life* and *nonlife* insurance. Life insurance relates to all perils associated with human life, while nonlife insurance covers the gamut of all else. Nonlife insurance is further divided into two categories: *property insurance* and *casualty insurance.*

Within the property insurance designation, there are several subcategories, including fire, and ocean marine, and inland marine insurance.

Fire Insurance

Fire insurance is an important part of an individual's protective coverage, since fires account for more unintended property destruction than any other single peril. Within insurance circles, fire is defined in one of two ways. First, a fire can be friendly in nature. That is, the fire is one that has been deliberately ignited and is intended to be contained within the designated boundaries. For example, a fire within a fireplace can be termed a friendly fire.

On the other hand, a hostile fire is one that is uncontrollable—one that rages beyond designated boundaries. For instance, the fireplace cited in the earlier example can also contain a hostile fire. If a strong downdraft causes the fire to leap from the fireplace, igniting a nearby couch, insurance would cover damages because of the unpredictability of the loss. However, if an item were thrown into the fireplace (where a friendly fire burned), an individual would not be compensated for a loss. In essence, insurance companies compensate for losses due to hostile fires, and it is up to the insurance professional to decide just when a friendly fire becomes a hostile one or when circumstances warrant payment for losses.

Often, associated perils are included in fire insurance coverage for individuals and businesses, with coverage including natural disasters and circumstances such as windstorms, hail, explosions, and smoke damage. In insurance parlance, these perils are tacked onto fire insurance coverage as extended-coverage endorsements.

Ocean Marine and Inland Marine Insurance

Ocean marine insurance is one of the oldest forms of insurance. Today, ocean marine insurance provides protection against a number of perils, including perils of the sea, war, and pirates. This type of all-inclusive protection is known as all-risk insurance, meaning that an insurance company must pay for losses regardless of the cause of losses. Logically, this type of protection is needed for seafaring vessels, since it would be difficult to determine what the cause of a loss would be if a ship sank to the bottom of the ocean.

Inland marine insurance is very similar to ocean marine insurance and practically was established as an outgrowth of the former type of security. Once cargoes began being transported through inland routes, individuals and merchants saw the need to insure goods traveling over land. Inland marine insurance differs from ocean marine insurance in several ways, though. The most important difference is that insurance companies may place certain requirements and specifications on losses and risks, since a company can easily investigate causes of losses that occur over land.

While property insurance covers the land and sea, casualty insurance blankets our country's legal system and the workplace. There are three divisions of casualty insurance: liability insurance, workers' compensation, and bonding.

Liability Insurance

Liability means responsibility; legal liability arises out of a general rule of law that an individual is responsible for any loss he or she may cause another to suffer. *Liability insurance* protects individuals from being sued by people they may have caused to suffer.

Law creates three categories of descriptions fitting situations where an individual injures another: civil wrongs done to another, breach of contract, and criminal wrongs. The area of liability insurance is highly complex, uniting several disciplines—including law and statistics—to determine negligence. Often, cases of liability result in lawsuit action taken up before courts. Liability insurance, in these cases, is used to pay court awards on cases regarding negligence.

Workers' Compensation

Like liability insurance, *workers' compensation* is used as a form of payment when an individual is responsible for another individual's loss. In workers' compensation cases, however, the "individual" responsible is a place of employment, while the person using the liability system is an employed worker.

For example, if a worker is injured while performing job duties at a workplace, legal liability falls on the employer to provide compensation for the injured employee. Through the use of workers' compensation, an employer may compensate the employee, paying medical and rehabilitative expenses, while providing financial support for the recuperating worker.

Employers often use this form of insurance to ensure that injuries in the workplace do not result in lawsuits. Like the legal liability insurance system, insurance companies providing workers' compensation programs must investigate for possible negligence, determining if a party was at fault in a situation. Such determinations then affect the outcome of provisions and reimbursements. Still, there need not be negligence to collect workers' compensation. It is a statutory system to "insure" workers.

Bonding

Of the three majors forms of casualty insurance, *bonding* is perhaps the most specialized. A bond is an agreement among three parties. One party is the bonding company, while the second is an individual committed to working for the third party.

There are two major branches of bonding: *fidelity bonding* and *surety bonding.* In a fidelity bond, the bond company agrees to pay the third party for losses caused by the dishonesty of the second party. In surety bonding, the bonding company (or surety) guarantees the performance of the second party to the third party.

Automobile Insurance

Within the realm of property and casualty insurance, a hybrid exists—*automobile insurance.* Automobile insurance merges the best aspects of the two forms of nonlife insurance, providing basic security regarding property (the automobile), while ensuring legal liability protection for incidents occurring from the operation of the motor vehicle. Because of the increasing number of automobiles on the roads of America, automobile insurance in recent decades has become a prevalent segment of the overall insurance industry.

Life Insurance

Insurance reduces uncertainty about loss. While death is not an uncertainty, the time of death is. And when death occurs before an individual has completed a career, it is thought of in insurance terms as a premature death. *Life insurance* provides protection for the financial loss most often associated with premature death.

Another aspect of life insurance regards the exhaustion of one's income at old age. A policy called an *annuity* establishes a contingency for this sort of situation, providing an individual with a regular income as long as he or she remains alive. Thus, while life insurance guarantees that an individual leaves an estate as financial assistance for her or his dependents (or beneficiaries), an annuity guarantees that an individual cannot outlive an estate.

Health Insurance

Usually placed under the category of life insurance, *health insurance* provides coverage for risks that are health related.

The disruption of a person's normal activities due to illness or injury produces two problems addressed by the insurance world: medical expenses, such as physician and hospital fees, and lost income while an individual is unable to work. Health insurance assists the individual in both instances.

There are three basic types of health insurance coverage: medical expense insurance, major medical insurance, and disability income insurance.

First, *medical expense insurance* includes coverage known as basic hospitalization. This type of insurance provides a payment for many services rendered by a physician, as well as most hospital expenses. Thus it protects the insured from financial loss due to medical costs. With most policies, the benefits are paid directly to the provider of the services rendered after bills are submitted by a physician or hospital. This way, the consumer is spared the financial burden of first paying for services and later filing with an insurance provider for reimbursement.

Second, *major medical insurance* provides coverage for the cost of serious illnesses. While this type of insurance covers major illnesses, it is often used in conjunction with medical expense insurance to provide more comprehensive coverage. In truth, major medical insurance is designed to provide protection for potentially large medical expenses and often is continued after basic medical expense insurance benefits have been exhausted.

Deductibles are often used in major medical insurance. With a deductible, the insured must pay a certain amount of a medical expense before major medical insurance begins to pay medical expenses. In addition, the insurer pays a percentage of the medical expenses, with the insured agreeing to pay the remainder. Typically, the insurer pays 75 to 80 percent of the medical expenses.

Finally, *disability income insurance* is designed to provide payments to compensate for lost wages due to sickness or in a period of disability. These policies are either short-term or long-term policies, depending on the length of protection offered.

Short-term policies provide a specific number of weeks of coverage, after a brief waiting period. The waiting period is a period of time, called an elimination period, that must elapse before insurance payments can begin. The purpose of the elimination period is to avoid making any payments for minor illnesses. Unlike short-term disability income insurance, long-term disability income insurance provides a number of years' protection, after a much more substantial elimination period.

Some policies include protection for partial disability, providing payments for a person who works part-time while recovering from an illness. In these cases, the payments make up the difference between the individual's part-time wages and the wages he or she would have earned working full-time.

Disability income insurance is available to individuals at different premium rates that are based on the age, sex, and health of the applicant. This type of insurance is also available as an extra cost provision to a life insurance policy. This provision is called a disability income rider—a rider being any addition to the policy.

CHAPTER 2

TYPES OF INSURANCE CAREERS

Worthwhile careers of several types are available within the insurance industry for the right-minded individual. These positions offer the challenge of diverse duties and new experiences, while providing a stable source of income to the insurance practitioner.

The industry itself is booming. As technology advances, so do specialized insurance fields. Therefore, new technological fields mean more insurance possibilities—and career growth for the insurance professional.

For the purposes of this book, individual career positions have been broken down into two major categories—agency careers and company careers. In reviewing the various job descriptions, the reader will see that a number of positions in one category seem similar to positions in the other category. This is intentional, since both types of insurance systems learn and grow from one another. In essence, each system adapts positions to better reflect the needs and wants of the other system. The two systems work with each other continually. Because of this, career positions tend to overlap.

Still, these positions stress different responsibilities within the context of the respective systems. That is, within the scheme and structure of an insurance company, a position provides different benefits than would a similar position within an agency.

An individual would be well-advised to investigate the intricacies of a specific company or agency before assuming that the position responsibilities described below can be applied to a particular job opening. Thus, the career descriptions in this chapter are meant as a basic guide to the types of responsibilities an individual can expect within a position in an agency or company environment.

AGENCY CAREERS

Sales

Within an agency setting, several individuals are responsible for maximizing sales production while affording the best possible service to agency clients. In essence, these *sales representatives* are the backbone of the agency, bringing in clients and servicing existing accounts.

There are several levels of sales personnel within the catch-all title of *producer,* with varying degrees of responsibilities.

First, account producers seek out new business, bringing clients to the agency. These individuals usually have a fair amount of experience in the insurance industry. They ensure that all services provided by the agency are performed properly, following up on all aspects of a client's account.

Account producers need to know intimately the workings of the agency, tracking every aspect of client service. In addition, account producers must have an understanding of their clients' businesses in order to provide the insurance protection that is necessary for successful operations.

Account producers also follow up on client claims, seeking the most equitable situation for their client. In truth, account producers represent the agency—they are the client's image of the agency.

Account producers typically must have a baccalaureate degree and should have prior experience in the insurance industry. The producers need strong verbal and interpersonal skills, given the high amount of client contact they have on a daily basis. They also need strong written communications skills in order to communicate with clients and insurance companies.

Account producers spend a great deal of their time in a conservative office environment. As a result, good grooming is essential for all producers, considering the fact that the public often sees in them the image of the agency. In truth, to some individuals the producer *is* the agency. Therefore, a neat, well-dressed individual often succeeds at producing new business.

While the producer often works in the agency's office, he or she may do some traveling while working on new accounts. It isn't uncommon to find a producer making personal calls on a prospective client, whether the call is at the prospective client's business, home, or a mutually agreed-upon setting.

Salary scales for producers vary from agency to agency but, on the average, a producer could expect a starting salary between $35,000 and $60,000. In addition, producers make a commission from new and maintained client accounts.

Like the producer, the *account executive* is responsible for the acquisition of new accounts and servicing existing clients. The account executive tracks the account, making sure that services and functions are performed properly. In essence, the account executive's responsibilities mirror the producer's—with one exception. An account executive generally has less experience than the producer. Therefore, the account executive is usually in a subordinate position to the producer.

The account executive often assumes the producer's full responsibilities when the producer is out of the office. In this way, there is always an individual on hand to service a client's account, affording the client the utmost in service.

An account executive must have a baccalaureate degree with prior experience in the insurance industry, working in some insurance capacity. Account executives must also possess an ability to analyze in-depth problems in order to understand the complexities of a client's needs. The account executive ideally possesses strong verbal, interpersonal, and written communications skills.

Generally, account executives can expect a starting salary between $20,000 and $30,000, depending on the amount of prior experience they possess.

Overseeing both producers and account executives, the *senior vice president* of sales encourages active solicitation of business. The senior vice president works with the producers and account executives on current client accounts and actively works on client account renewals. In addition, the senior vice president oversees expenses and determines salaries and fringe benefits of sales producers.

The senior vice president typically works in an office, but also works in the field, visiting clients to ensure that their accounts are being handled properly.

A baccalaureate degree is required of a senior vice president, as well as extensive sales experience as a producer or account executive. Generally, the senior vice president can expect a salary between $35,000 and $75,000, depending on work experience.

Claims Representative

Within the agency hierarchy, the *claims representative* is responsible for the day-to-day duties stemming from property, casualty, workers' compensation, and auto claims, acting as a liaison between the insurance company and clients settling claims. (Various levels of claims personnel are also utilized by insurance companies. Thus, the following claims positions described within the context of agency careers also are company positions.)

The claims representative takes claims information from clients who experience a loss, but can also receive this type of information from producers. Then, the claims representative transfers claim information to the appropriate insurance company department via the telephone or written communications. In addition, the claims representative enters all claims information into the agency's computer or file system in order to maintain a record of all claims for other agency personnel.

Beyond taking such information, the claims representative prepares files on active claims and issues agency checks to the insured.

Claims representatives must possess strong verbal, interpersonal, and written communications skills in order to deal effectively with clients. Typically, the claims representative works in an office with limited public contact.

The claims representative ideally has a high school (or equivalent) education, although a baccalaureate degree is preferred. In addition, the claims representative should have prior insurance industry experience.

The claims representative can expect a starting salary within the $15,000 to $30,000 range, depending on the individual's experience.

Claims Manager

The *claims manager* is responsible for setting priorities on tasks and delegating them to the claims representative. In addition, the claims manager reviews losses with producers and processes property, casualty, and auto claims.

The claims manager's responsibilities include reporting all levels of losses for clients to assigned insurance companies, following up with insurance companies for claims payments or additional information, appealing claims on behalf of clients, advising clients on terms of various policies, and managing claims representatives.

Claims managers must possess strong verbal, interpersonal, and written communications skills and must have the ability to organize, set priorities, and delegate tasks. In addition, the claims manager must be able to work without close supervision. Typically, the claims manager works in an office.

Claims managers are required to have baccalaureate degrees and must possess prior claim and management experience. Starting salaries range from $25,000 to $40,000, depending on experience.

Claims Examiner

The *claims examiner* is responsible for the processing of group medical, dental, and vision claims for the benefits division of an insurance agency.

The claims examiner's responsibilities include determining appropriate benefit levels in accordance with policy provisions, servicing accounts, and communicating client problems through appropriate lines of communication.

Claims examiners must possess a knowledge of medical terminology and must demonstrate strong verbal and written communications skills. Examiners must also be able to organize assignments and set priorities. Typically, the claims examiner works in an office, investigating claims via phone work.

Claims examiners must possess a high school (or equivalent) education, although a college education is preferred. In addition, prior experience in group insurance is required.

Claims examiners can expect starting salaries between $17,000 and $25,000, depending on experience.

Benefits Claims Manager

The *benefits claims manager* is responsible for supervising the examination and investigation of claims, while acting as a liaison between claims examiners, clients, and producers.

A benefits claims manager's duties include the training of new personnel, assisting in the redesign of health care plans, acting as a customer relations advocate, and maintaining claim histories of clients.

Benefits claims managers must possess strong written, verbal, and interpersonal communications skills, as well as the ability to manage others in a work environment.

A baccalaureate degree is required for a position as a benefits claims manager, as well as prior insurance and management experience. Starting salaries range between $24,000 and $35,000, depending on experience.

Marketing Representatives

Marketing representatives work in all lines of insurance—personal lines, commercial (business) lines, and benefits—quoting and underwriting different types of insurance.

In addition, the marketing representative's duties include completing applications for new orders, processing cancellation notices, preparing billing orders, recommending the proper policy forms to clients, analyzing hypothetical situations, and conducting audits of client insurance policies.

Marketing representatives must possess a knowledge of policy forms and coverages. In addition, the representative must have strong financial, mathematical, and writing skills. A baccalaureate degree is required, as well as knowledge of the insurance industry. Prior experience in insurance is also required.

Salaries range from $18,000 to $30,000, depending on experience.

POSITIONS IN INSURANCE COMPANIES

Actuary

Within the insurance company, the *actuary* is a highly respected figure. Actuaries deal with the statistical, financial, and mathematical calculations involving the probability of future payment of insurance plans. They, in essence, determine rates for premiums based on the amount of risk involved.

Actuaries study the frequency of hurricanes, fires, tornadoes, thefts, explosions, and other similar disasters. They tabulate the damage caused by such incidents, using the data to assume financial damages. Using this information, they then calculate the probability of these types of events occurring again. The actuary then recommends the premium prices that should be charged for insurance to protect against these events (risks).

Actuaries must have a keen sense of mathematics and must display financial skills. A baccalaureate degree, preferably in the actuarial sciences or finance, is required of the actuary. Actuaries usually work in an office and have little or no client contact.

Starting salaries range from $25,000 to $35,000, depending on experience. Mid-range salaries can be as high as $45,000 to $50,000, with top salaries over $60,000.

Agents

Agents act primarily as salespeople for their company, soliciting clients and new prospects. Once an agent contacts the prospective client, he or she explains the various services of the company and develops insurance plans for the client. Once the client agrees to insurance coverage, the agent acts on behalf of the company, servicing the client.

Agents, for the most part, must aggressively seek out these clients. Companies often place a quota on the number of prospective clients an agent must contact. For instance, a company may ask that agents make thirty calls a week to potential clients. Of these thirty calls, an agent may interview ten interested individuals. In turn, these interviews may actually land only one or two clients. Clearly, individuals seeking a career as an insurance agent must have an optimistic attitude, as well as a gregarious personality.

Although a baccalaureate degree is desirable, an interested individual with a high school education may enter the field as an agent. Often, companies provide training programs for their agents, introducing them to the nuances of the company and insurance procedures.

Salaries for insurance agents vary. Because the agent works mostly on a commission basis, aggressive agents can virtually decide on their salary. It is not uncommon for an agent to make from $40,000 to $85,000 a year, if he or she actively seeks out clients. On the other hand, becoming an insurance agent could be financially ruinous for individuals who do not apply themselves to the rigors of client contact.

Agents often work in an environment that affords them public contact, in communities and centers of metropolitan business. The environment is most often pleasant and can be diverse—agents can work in storefront offices or huge office buildings. They clearly venture to where the public is, using their personal traits to gain access to new markets.

Field Representatives

Within the insurance industry, a *field representative* is an individual who acts as a liaison between the insurance company and the agents who sell the insurance company's policies. Field representatives provide the agent with a vital link to the company, updating procedures and policies for the agent to follow within the course of her or his day-to-day dealings with the public.

Most often, a field representative's responsibilities include making sure agents fully understand developments within the company, advising agents with regard to sales and the servicing of customers, and describing new policies. Because of this, the field representative must have an intimate knowledge of the insurance company and the insurance field in general.

Field representatives usually travel a great deal, checking on company agents at various locations. Because of their contact with agents, these representatives must possess keen verbal and interpersonal skills. A baccalaureate degree is often required of field representatives and almost certainly is a requirement for advancement in the field. Many insurance company presidents and top-level executives began their careers as field representatives for a company, learning the various facets of insurance work in the field.

Starting salaries range from $28,000 to $40,000, depending on experience.

Underwriters

Underwriters most often make decisions on behalf of a company as to the acceptance or rejection of applications for insurance. Working with actuarial data, the underwriter determines whether a potential client is a proper risk, given the type of insurance requested. In addition, the underwriter determines what rates a client should pay for insurance, based on the amount of risk involved with insuring the client.

Because the insurance business is highly competitive, the underwriter's job is crucial to the success of a company. For instance, if an underwriter quotes a premium price that is too low, the company can lose funds over a period of time. On the other hand, if the underwriter quotes too high a price, the company may lose a prospective client to a competitor who offers lower prices. For these reasons, underwriters must possess sound judgment and a strong business sense.

Underwriters work in offices. A baccalaureate degree is preferred. In addition, the underwriter should have extensive insurance experience.

Underwriter trainees—individuals learning the underwriting business—can expect starting salaries from $20,000 to $30,000. Senior underwriters can expect starting salaries up to $50,000.

Adjusters

Insurance adjusters, often called claims investigators, are responsible for determining whether losses are covered by an insurance company. In addition, they determine the financial amount of the losses in order to provide financial payment for losses.

Adjusters can work with many diverse types of claims, ranging from automobile accidents to crop damage, from stolen goods to fire damage. They can also be specialists, working with only one type of claim, such as vehicle damage.

Adjusters work in a number of environments. Some adjusters rush to the scenes of disasters and accidents, such as tornadoes and hurricanes. Others work in an office, reviewing claims as they are reported to the company. Because the adjuster has a high amount of contact with the public, he or she must have strong verbal and interpersonal skills. In addition, the adjuster must possess strong written communication skills in order to convey loss information to company officials and clients.

Although a baccalaureate degree is not required of an adjuster, it is preferred. Since adjusters must be able to explain to policyholders the legal technicalities of insurance contracts, a knowledge of law is also useful. In addition, the adjuster must have an extensive knowledge of the insurance field.

Adjusters can expect starting salaries between $25,000 and $35,000 per year.

Loss Control Specialists

Loss control specialists envision, develop, and implement safety programs that hold accidents to a minimum—thus, controlling losses. These specialists survey work areas and operations, identify hazards, and make recommendations on the elimination of potential hazards.

Loss control specialists work with executives of industrial firms and public institutions, as well as city managers, attempting to correct harmful situations. For this reason, they travel often.

Loss control specialists are required to have a baccalaureate degree, as well as prior insurance work experience. In addition, specialists should have a knowledge of safety procedures, engineering, and occupational health.

Individuals interested in a career as a loss control specialist may expect starting salaries between $22,000 and $30,000 per year.

Cost Containment Specialists

Cost containment specialists work closely with sales personnel and clients to design specialized health care cost management programs for employee benefits plans. (In some cases, insurance agencies have a cost containment specialist on staff, but most often they hire consultants who work with them.)

Cost containment specialists work most often in an office, but travel to hospitals and other health care providers, setting up hospital cost containment programs and learning new cost containment programs.

Cost containment specialists must possess a baccalaureate degree. An advanced degree in health care administration is preferred. In addition, cost containment specialists must have an extensive knowledge of health care and employee benefits programs.

Cost containment specialists can expect a starting salary between $35,000 and $55,000, depending on their experience.

CHAPTER 3

EDUCATION AND TRAINING

Because insurance is a complex topic, some type of education or specialized training is generally necessary to succeed in the field. This may consist of job experience, formal education, or a combination of the two.

Many positions within the insurance industry are based on prior experience. In some cases, experience is the best educator.

During the early years of the insurance industry, many positions were created through trial and error. For instance, when one person's workload became too difficult to handle, someone else was assigned to various aspects of that individual's functions. Offshoots of job responsibilities created new positions—an adaptation of sorts.

Jobs became more fragmented, with people assuming more specialized roles within an organization. Indeed, the insurance professional who once handled many aspects of a claim now has individuals assisting her or him. Many of these individuals received their positions—and the additional duties assigned to these positions—through actual work experience.

However, as technology advances and the insurance industry becomes more regulated, chances that an individual can achieve great success without a systemized education begin to fade. Work experience is an important factor in acceptance to the field, and promotions most often occur to those individuals who persevere, logging in years of experience. But nothing beats a solid education.

If a student feels that work experience is a viable route, here is a word of advice: Seek out an internship opportunity while in school. An internship is a form of education in which an individual actually works part-time (or full-time, depending on the arrangement) at a company, agency, or association in the field, acquiring school credit for the tasks performed while at the firm.

Most often, the internship lasts a school semester and provides valuable experience for the student. The internship's employer, in turn, often gets an eager worker for a semester. A list of associations that may be able to put you in touch with organizations in your area is featured in the chapter in this book on associations (Chapter 6).

The student usually must initiate an internship process, contacting an employer in the area to work on ironing out credit details. In addition, the student may want to contact a school counselor to ease the process. Some schools even have established internship departments or programs.

Although internships provide valuable experience, today's student must be well-rounded to compete in the career opportunity marketplace. Since the insurance industry is a wider field than, say, accountancy, where the balancing of numbers takes up most of a professional's workday, a broad education is recommended.

It would help a student to remember that most insurance positions entail several different disciplines. During a given day, an insurance professional may talk with consumers, balance numbers, and work out legalities. Thus, the insurance professional needs service (people) skills, mathematical aptitude, and analytical ability. The only way to get that—and get ahead—is a concentration on a broad range of scholastic subjects.

HIGH SCHOOL BACKGROUND

To obtain the proper "people" skills, a student must interact with a great number of diverse individuals, learning to cope with differing personalities. In a way, the student has done it, unconsciously, for most of her or his life—talking to friends, meeting new people, attending school. Still, interactive skills can be improved through public speaking courses, English courses, and perhaps drama courses. Such studies force the student to make presentations before classmates and instructors and help the student refine speaking skills. At the same time, such courses serve to build a student's self-confidence in communication abilities, an important need in the service-oriented world of insurance.

While strong communication skills are important, many types of insurance careers involve mathematics or mathematical principles. Rates, premiums, policies—even risks—are based on mathematics. It would serve the student well to get an early start on what will be a lifetime of working with numbers.

Other subjects are also useful to students who are considering a position in insurance. Social studies provides the student with an understanding of societal needs. History classes make the student keenly aware of the impact certain events have on the economy. Foreign language courses provide a valuable communications tool. In sum, no subjects should be neglected as being outside the realm of this career choice.

Ideally, a student considering a career in insurance should take the following course load:

- Three to four units of mathematics
- Three to four units of English
- One unit of public speaking
- One to two units of a common foreign language, such as Spanish or German
- One to two units of social studies
- One to two units of history
- One to two units of computer course work
- Word processing courses

Although this is an ideal situation—to create a well-rounded curriculum—the student should be aware that all courses in some way pertain to life and, in turn, to the selection of a career.

EDUCATION AFTER HIGH SCHOOL

More and more employers are requiring prospective job applicants to have a college or university education. On one level, such an education shows prospective employers the seriousness of the job applicant—a college degree entails hard work and is not undertaken by someone with no sense of personal direction. On another level, such advanced education polishes skills that are learned early on. With the scarcity of employment positions in these times, college graduates have a definite edge over those individuals who don't have such a formal education.

The advice given to a high school student—taking diverse courses to become more well-rounded—applies to the college student as well. A liberal arts education consisting of a smattering of different disciplines helps to shape the student's view of herself or himself and of the world. And it affects the attitude taken toward the world later in a career.

While the student should concentrate on a diverse education, he or she should also take advantage of the range of specialized courses available. For instance, statistical courses translate well toward an insurance career, as do courses in economics. Advanced mathematics courses help the student refine computational skills, while writing courses help students learn to organize their thoughts. All these skills are needed to assist the public and carry on business within the insurance realm.

Business courses are also a worthy addition to a college student's course load. The principles expounded upon in these courses can be directly applied within the course of a single day working in the insurance field. Those individuals who have a firm grasp of business principles also have a greater chance of promotions.

In recent years, schools have found that insurance is a scholastic field unto itself. For that reason, a number of universities, colleges, and community colleges have established full curricula in insurance. For example, insurance courses offered by Colorado's Regis College include the following:

- *Property and Liability Insurance Principles (INS 200).* Covers basic principles of insurance, introduction to contracts, and operations of insurance business.
- *Personal Insurance.* Deals with analysis of personal loss exposures and personal insurance coverages, including home, auto, life, and health.
- *Commercial Insurance.* Deals with commercial coverages such as property, business income, inland and ocean marine, crime, boiler and machinery, general liability, auto, workers' compensation, and package policies.
- *Delivering Insurance Services.* Applies the principles of Total Quality Management (T.Q.M.) as they apply to the delivery of insurance service.
- *The Claims Environment.* Covers topics related to how the claim representative's role is simultaneously determined by policyholders and other customers, the insurance policy, the insurance company and its management, and the law.
- *Workers' Compensation and Medical Aspects of Claims.* Explains the workers' compensation system and its problems.

- *Property Loss Adjusting.* Deals with apportionment, insurable interest, limitations on the amount of insurer's liability, and adjustment of various types of losses.
- *Liability Claim Adjusting.* Examines the law of contracts, torts, agency, bailments, products, automobiles, evidence, and damages. Includes introduction to medical knowledge.
- *Essentials of Risk Management.* Focuses on initial steps in the risk management decision-making process.
- *Essentials of Risk Control.* Covers additional steps in the risk management process.
- *Essentials of Risk Financing.* Completes the examination of the risk management decision-making process.
- *Ethics, Insurance Perspectives, and Insurance Contract.* Covers the risk management framework, the insurance environment, and principles of insurance contract analysis.
- *Personal Insurance and Risk Management.* Deals with risk management of individual and family exposures.
- *Commercial Property Insurance and Risk Management.* Covers analysis and measurement of commercial loss exposures and insurance coverages designed to meet those exposures.
- *Commercial Liability Risk Management and Insurance.* Covers major sources of liability loss exposure and applicable controls and the insurance coverages designed to meet such exposures.
- *Insurance Operations.* Examines insurance marketing, underwriting, reinsurance, rate making, claims adjusting, loss control activities, and other functions and activities.

- *The Legal Environment of Insurance.* Covers general business law in areas such as tort, contract, and agency law and application of business law to insurance.
- *Personal Insurance Underwriting and Marketing Practices.* Addresses topics such as product delivery and underwriting, customer perceptions, and risk selection marketing exposures.
- *Personal Insurance: Services, Management, and Issues.* Covers customer relations, price development, social and regulatory issues, and related topics.
- *Commercial Liability Underwriting.* Deals with major lines of commercial liability insurance with emphasis on underwriting and risk classification.
- *Commercial Property and Multiple Lines Underwriting.* Covers commercial property risks including analyzing loss, frequency and severity of fire and other perils, indirect losses and marine risks.

A well-known school specializing in insurance is the College of Insurance, located in New York City. This is a four-year institution of higher education where students study insurance, risk management, financial services, and actuarial science as well as the liberal arts.

The College of Insurance offers the following degrees:

- Bachelor of Business Administration
- Bachelor of Science
- Master of Business Administration
- Master of Science in Risk Management
- Associate in Occupational Studies

For information about admissions or other matters, contact:

The College of Insurance
101 Murray Street
New York, NY 10007

Many other colleges and universities also offer insurance courses. Typically, the number of courses available is smaller than that of schools specializing in insurance instruction. For example, Southwest Missouri State University offers the following insurance courses:

- *Insurance.* An overview of property, casualty, and life insurance with applications in both personal and business situations.
- *Life Insurance.* A look at the nature and types of life insurance and annuity contracts.
- *Property and Liability Insurance.* Covers analysis and application of risk and insurance principles to direct and consequential losses.
- *Employee Benefits and Social Insurance.* Deals with group life and health insurance, retirement programs, Social Security, and other social insurance programs.
- *Insurance Topics.* Intensifies and supplements the study of insurance including property/casualty, risk management, life/health, employee benefits, financial services, and insurance-related areas.
- *Risk Management.* Covers loss exposures and alternative techniques for treating each exposure.

Those students who are convinced they would like to enter the insurance field are urged to investigate the possibility of studying toward a degree with emphasis on insurance course work. Following is a list of some schools with insurance curricula:

University of Alabama
  Tuscaloosa, AL 35401
  (205) 348-5121

Appalachian State University
  Boone, NC 28608
  (704) 262-2000

Arizona State University
  Tempe, AZ 85287
  (602) 965-9011

University of Arkansas
  Fayetteville, AR 72701
  (501) 575-2000

Bowling Green State University
  Bowling Green, OH 43403
  (419) 372-2531

Casper College
  125 College Drive
  Casper, WY 82601
  (307) 268-2110

Central Texas College
  US Highway 190 West
  Killeen, TX 76540
  (817) 526-7161

University of Cincinnati
    Cincinnati, OH 45221
    (513) 556-6000

City University of New York
    Bernard M. Baruch College
    17 Lexington Avenue
    New York, NY 10010
    (212) 802-2000

City University of New York
    Queensborough Community College
    Springfield Boulevard and Fifty-Sixth Avenue
    Bayside, NY 11364
    (212) 631-6262

Clarion University of Pennsylvania
    Clarion, PA 16214
    (814) 226-2000

The College of Insurance
    One Insurance Plaza
    101 Murray Street
    New York, NY 10007
    (212) 962-4111

University of Connecticut
    Storrs, CT 06269
    (860) 486-2000

Drake University
    Twenty-Fifth Street and University Avenue
    Des Moines, IA 50311
    (515) 271-2011

Eastern Kentucky University
  Richmond, KY 40475-0931
  (606) 622-1000

Florida State University
  Tallahassee, FL 32306
  (850) 644-2525

University of Florida
  Gainesville, FL 32611
  (352) 392-3261

Gadsden State Community College
  Wallace Drive
  Gadsden, AL 35902
  (205) 549-8200

University of Hartford
  200 Bloomfield Avenue
  West Hartford, CT 06117
  (860) 768-4100

Husson College
  1 College Circle
  Bangor, ME 04401
  (207) 947-7000

Hutchinson Community College
  1300 North Plum Street
  Hutchinson, KS 67501
  (316) 665-3500

Illinois Wesleyan University
  P. O. Box 2900
  Bloomington, IL 61702
  (309) 556-1000

Indiana University at Bloomington
    Bloomington, IN 47405
    (812) 855-4848

University of Iowa
    Iowa City, IA 52242
    (319) 335-3500

LaSalle University
    Olney Avenue and Twentieth Street
    Philadelphia, PA 19141
    (215) 951-1000

Mankato State University
    South Road and Ellis Avenue
    Mankato, MN 56002
    (507) 389-2463

The University of Memphis
    Memphis, TN 38152
    (901) 678-2000

Michigan State University
    East Lansing, MI 48824
    (517) 355-1855

MidAmerica Nazarene University
    2030 East College Way
    Olathe, KS 66062
    (913) 782-3750

Middle Tennessee State University
    Murfreesboro, TN 37132
    (615) 898-2300

Mohawk Valley Community College
1101 Sherman Drive
Utica, NY 13501
(315) 792-5400

University of Nevada, Las Vegas
4505 South Maryland Parkway
Las Vegas, NV 89154
(702) 895-3011

New Mexico State University
Las Cruces, NM 88003
(505) 646-0111

North Dakota State University
Fargo, ND 58105
(701) 231-8011

University of Northern Colorado
Greeley, CO 80639
(970) 351-1890

Oklahoma State University
Stillwater, OK 74078
(405) 744-5000

Olivet College
Olivet, MI 49076
(616) 749-7000

Pennsylvania State University
201 Old Main
University Park, PA 16802
(814) 865-4700

University of Rhode Island
  Kingston, RI 02881
  (401) 874-1000

St. Mary's University
  1 Camino Santa Maria
  San Antonio, TX 78228
  (210) 436-3011

University of South Carolina
  Columbia, SC 29208
  (803) 777-7700

University of Southern Mississippi
  Southern Station Box 5167
  Hattiesburg, MS 39406
  (601) 266-4111

Thomas Edison State College
  101 West State Street
  Trenton, NJ 08608
  (609) 984-1000

Washington State University
  2580 N.E. Grimes Way
  Pullman, WA 99164
  (509) 335-3564

In addition to the schools offering insurance course work for students, a number of colleges and universities offer curricula in actuarial sciences. The actuarial sciences involve the specific application of mathematical and statistical principles to rate-making within insurance. Following is a list of those schools offering curricula in the actuarial sciences:

Ball State University
  Muncie, IN 47306
  (765) 289-1241

Butler University
  Forty-Sixth at Sunset Avenue
  Indianapolis, IN 46208
  (317) 940-8000

University of Cincinnati
  Cincinnati, OH 45221
  (513) 556-6000

University of Connecticut
  Storrs, CT 06269
  (860) 486-2000

Drake University
  Twenty-Fifth Street and University Avenue
  Des Moines, IA 50311
  (515) 271-2011

Georgia State University
  University Plaza
  Atlanta, GA 30303-3083
  (404) 651-2000

University of Hartford
  200 Bloomfield Avenue
  West Hartford, CT 06117-0395
  (860) 768-4100

University of Iowa
  Iowa City, IA 52242
  (319) 335-3500

Lebanon Valley College
  Annville, PA 17003-0501
  (717) 867-6100

Maryville College
  Maryville, TN 37804
  (423) 981-8000

University of Michigan
  Ann Arbor, MI 48109
  (313) 764-1817

University of Minnesota, Twin Cities
  Minneapolis, MN 55455
  (612) 625-5000

University of Nebraska
  Fourteenth and R Streets
  Lincoln, NE 68588
  (402) 472-7211

University of North Carolina, Chapel Hill
  Chapel Hill, NC 27599
  (919) 962-2211

Ohio State University
  Columbus, OH 43210-1358
  (614) 292-6446

Oregon State University
  Corvallis, OR 97331
  (541) 737-0123

Pennsylvania State University
  201 Old Main
  University Park, PA 16802
  (814) 865-4700

University of Pennsylvania
  Thirty-Fourth and Spruce Street
  Philadelphia, PA 19104
  (215) 898-5000

Roosevelt University
  430 South Michigan Avenue
  Chicago, IL 60605-1394
  (312) 341-3500

State University of New York, Buffalo
  Buffalo, NY 14260
  (716) 645-2000

Temple University
  Philadelphia, PA 19122
  (215) 204-7000

University of Wisconsin, Madison
  500 Lincoln Drive
  Madison, WI 53706
  (608) 262-1234

CHAPTER 4

GETTING LICENSED

The insurance industry is a vital part of the nation's economy. Recognizing its importance, state agencies and the federal government impose licensing regulations on the insurance industry and on professionals working within it. These regulations are imposed for a variety of reasons, all stemming from a concern for the consumer's welfare.

A major reason the industry is regulated, through the licensing of individuals in insurance sales, is to maintain certain economic forces. Because the insurance industry has an effect on the nation's economy, and vice versa, measures must be enacted and monitored to ensure that events within the industry don't cause wild fluctuations in the economy.

To fully understand the need for regulatory licensing, one must look at an example at the state, or local, level. For instance, the bankruptcy of an insurance company through shoddy practices by unlicensed sales workers can cause great harm to the citizens of a state in more ways than one. First, the premiums collected from individuals and businesses would no longer benefit the economy, because the insurance company couldn't reinvest funds to maintain solvency.

More important, the bankruptcy affects other businesses, many of which cannot function without insurance. If an insurance company becomes bankrupt, smaller businesses, which need insurance to survive in the marketplace, will follow suit. Once these smaller businesses enter bankruptcy, larger businesses, who often need the small businesses for parts, manufactured items, or other services, will be hard pressed to continue doing business. Thus, the elimination of one insurance company eventually causes irreparable harm to the state's economy, creating a ripple effect throughout the state.

This type of example can also be applied to the national economy, since the nation's economy is comprised of state economies. If businesses in one state begin shutting down because of a lack of insurance, the effects would be felt in surrounding states that use the resources of the faltering state. It would take only several statewide ripples to actually create waves nationwide.

There is another important reason regulations are imposed on the insurance industry—licensing is required of individuals working in insurance sales. Because consumers spend a sizable portion of their personal assets (over a great period of time) to ensure their own security, great care must be taken to work with consumers in their best interest. Without proper licensing, an unscrupulous individual may take advantage of the consumer's faith in the insurance system.

Because the consumer isn't always well versed in the complexities of insurance, the unlicensed sales worker could convince the consumer to apply for unneeded insurance policies. Such actions may spell financial disaster for the consumer.

For these reasons, state statutes prohibit any person from selling insurance without a license. In order to maintain licensing, stiff penalties are sometimes enacted by states to ensure that the industry polices itself. For example, Section 492.2 of the Illinois Insurance Law states that it is a misdemeanor for any individual or firm to act as an insurance agent or broker unless licensed. Even when an individual does have a license, he or she may not act as an agent for an insurance company that is not authorized or licensed to do business in the state where the prospective salesperson seeks a license.

Similarly, Section 507.1 of the Illinois Insurance Law states that no company licensed to operate in the state may pay commission to a person who is not licensed, further ensuring that the industry provides an environment for the licensing of salespersons.

Although state legislation often dictates licensing requirements for the insurance industry, in some cases, particular insurance companies or agencies also post special requirements of its sales force, above and beyond state regulations.

The state agency that regulates sales licensing is most often called the state insurance department. A commissioner or director generally heads the state department and is either appointed to the position by the governor or is duly elected. All insurance commissioners belong to a separate regulatory body called the National Association of Insurance Commissioners (NAIC). The association meets twice a year to discuss pertinent issues and formulate model bills pertaining to insurance matters. The model bills are often presented before each state legislature simultaneously, in an attempt to achieve uniformly proposed bills on insurance regulations. In effect, the National Association of Insurance Commissioners seeks to create a uniform insurance environment throughout the United States. However, state legislatures in the past have taken the model bills and used them only as frameworks for larger bill packages, tacking on amendments and changes and diminishing the strength of uniformity.

Following is a representation of the licensing requirements for salespersons in order to give an overview of licensing. You may contact your state insurance department or local office of the Independent Insurance Agents of America for more information on your state's specific requirements. A listing of the Independent Insurance Agents of America branch offices in major cities is included at the end of this chapter.

AGE REQUIREMENTS

The minimum age for holding an insurance license varies by state. In some states, licenses to sell individual types of insurance have different age requirements. Until recently, the minimum age in most states was twenty-one. However, changing laws dealing with majority age have caused many states to lower their minimum age requirement to eighteen.

APPLICATION REQUIREMENTS

Many states require the prospective salesperson to submit a written application for a license as well as a producer's bond to guarantee her or his future performance. A producer's bond is obtained from a surety company as a form of guarantee for a salesperson's performance in a prospective insurance company. Producer's bonds are available in predescribed sums starting at $2,500. If a prospective agent will be bringing in a great dollar amount of premiums, a high producer's bond fee is required. Likewise, if a prospective agent brings in small dollar amounts of premiums, a smaller producer's bond is required.

In addition, the insurance company that the applicant plans to represent must submit a certificate stating the company is satisfied that the applicant is trustworthy and competent. The insurance company must also state that the applicant will serve as the company's agent upon successful completion of all licensing requirements.

ACCREDITED COURSE WORK REQUIREMENTS

In some states, an applicant must pass a prescribed number of accredited insurance courses prior to taking the licensing examination. This requirement is intended to ensure that the applicant is properly prepared for the test. Certification that the applicant for a sales position has completed such course work is an ordinary part of the insurance company's filing responsibility with the state insurance department.

LICENSING EXAMINATIONS

All applicants for a license to sell insurance must successfully pass a licensing examination in their state. A certain fee, paid to the state insurance department, is required before taking the test.

For example, the state of Illinois requires an individual taking the licensing examination to pay $65 as a test fee for the licensing examination. In addition, the individual must pay $75 for the license upon successful completion of the examination. The individual must also pay for courses leading to the examination, often costing $200 or more per course. Finally, a licensed agent or salesperson must renew her or his license each year. The renewal cost per year in Illinois is $75.

The test format varies from state to state, but all cover the same basic material. For example, the Illinois Licensing Examination is made up of approximately three hundred multiple-choice questions that are broken down into three areas:

1. Life, Accident, and Health Insurance
2. Property and Casualty Insurance
3. Motor Vehicle Insurance

Although individuals can take selected sections of the test—opting to take only a motor vehicle insurance licensing examination, for example—most applicants take examinations for every section. This enables them to sell all types of insurance upon successful completion of licensing requirements.

The examinations themselves are broken down into sections, with each area of the examination consisting of a uniform section and a unique section. The uniform section of a particular examination area includes questions that were prepared by the National Association of Insurance Commissioners and are equally applicable to every state. Questions in the unique section of an examination pertain to individual state regulations and subjects that should be covered or given additional emphasis because of special circumstances in that state.

A licensing applicant should be prepared to respond to questions that evaluate three levels of insurance knowledge: recall—definitions of key words and phrases; comprehension—a full understanding of principles; and application—relating principles to problem-solving situations.

Prospective applicants often underestimate the complexity of a licensing examination and try to pass without intensive studies. However, the state licensing examinations cover insurance problems in depth. Following is an example showing the areas touched upon in a licensing examination section for property and casualty insurance agents.

**AREAS COVERED IN THE PROPERTY
AND CASUALTY EXAMINATION**

I. Principles of property and casualty insurance
   A. Importance of insurance
   B. Definitions
   C. Characteristics of insurance
     1. Probability
     2. Characteristics of an insurable risk
   D. Classification of companies
   E. Insurance company functions

II. Legal aspects of property and casualty insurance

III. The policy
   A. Parts of the policy including declarations and conditions
   B. Rate making
   C. Coverage
     1. Named peril vs. all risk
     2. Items covered by the policy
     3. Losses
   D. Limitations on recovery
     1. Actual cash value and depreciation
     2. Co-insurance
     3. Uses and types of deductibles
     4. Occupancy limitations
     5. Policy limits
     6. Repair or total loss
   E. Notice and proof of loss
     1. Details to be provided

2. Duty to protect
3. Cooperation clauses
4. Appraisal clauses
5. Time limits on lawsuits
6. Claim settlements

IV. Considerations pertaining to types of insurance
  A. Fire insurance
    1. Friendly vs. hostile fires
    2. Ignition
    3. Lightning
    4. Consequential loss
  B. Marine insurance
    1. Ocean marine insurance
    2. Inland marine insurance
  C. Liability Insurance
    1. Types of torts
    2. Negligence
    3. Malpractice
    4. Products liability
  D. Personal and commercial packages
    1. Homeowner's policy
    2. Farmowner's policy
    3. Commercial packages
  E. Automobile insurance
    1. Legislation affecting operation
    2. Assigned risk plans
    3. Safe driver plans
    4. Premium rate determination
  F. Theft insurance

G. Bonds
   1. Fidelity bonds
   2. Bonds for banks
   3. Surety bonds
   4. Contract bonds
H. Aviation insurance
V. Specific insurance policies and forms
   A. Fire insurance policies (boiler and machinery insurance)
   B. Marine insurance policies
   C. Liability insurance policies
   D. Personal and commercial package policies
   E. Automobile policies
   F. Theft insurance policies
      1. Personal theft policies
      2. Business theft policies
      3. Bank theft policies
      4. Forgery insurance policies
   G. Bond policies
      1. Commercial fidelity bonds
      2. Three-D policies
      3. Bank bond policies
      4. Surety bond policies
   H. Aviation insurance policies
      1. Hull policies
      2. Liability insurance coverage
VI. State and federal government mandated coverage
   A. Workers' compensation
   B. Federal riot reinsurance

    C. Federal flood insurance
    D. Federal crime insurance
VII. Government supervision and licensing
    A. State and federal regulations
    B. Ethical conduct
    C. Rate regulation

Certainly, a prospective applicant cannot go into an examination with an indifferent attitude. A position in the insurance field is, in all actuality, a career. When an individual makes a career choice in the insurance industry, personal commitment is definitely a must.

Because of a licensing test's complexity, some states put a limit on the number of times an applicant can take the test without passing it. If the applicant is unable to pass the exam after the predescribed number of attempts, he or she has to wait until a specified amount of time elapses. In some states, the applicant may be unable to take the test again after a specified number of attempts.

CONTINUING EDUCATION REQUIREMENTS

Following the successful completion of the licensing examination, many states require a licensee to continue her or his insurance education at an accredited institution. For example, an Illinois licensee is required to complete twenty-five hours of accredited insurance course work each year for four years after passing the exam.

TEMPORARY LICENSES

In some instances, certain states allow a person to obtain a temporary license to sell insurance. This authority is limited to the following:

1. Individuals who are selling insurance in the presence of a fully licensed agent.
2. Individuals who handle only business renewals and premium collections. This may include a person who is the administrator or executor of a deceased person's estate or the next-of-kin of a disabled agent.
3. Individuals who are hired by a firm and are undergoing a sales training program. In this case, individuals are not allowed to countersign insurance policies. In addition, they must be under continual supervision by the firm they will represent, and they must agree to take the permanent license examination on a scheduled date.

TERMINATING LICENSES

When a license to sell insurance is terminated, there is usually mutual consent between the agent and the insurance company he or she represents. In this type of case, when no violations occur, it is the insurer's responsibility to return the license to the state insurance department.

However, instances do arise that give the insurance department the authority to revoke or suspend the license of any individual. For example, Section 501.1 of the Illinois Insurance Law allows the state to revoke or suspend a person's license after notice and a hearing, if the agent does any of the following:

1. Is found guilty of fraudulent or dishonest practices
2. Misappropriates funds or illegally withholds monies
3. Demonstrates lack of trustworthiness or competence
4. Is convicted of a felony and fails to demonstrate sufficient rehabilitation to warrant public trust

AGENCIES TO CONTACT
FOR MORE INFORMATION

Following is a state-by-state list of agencies to contact regarding licensing requirements.

Alabama

Alabama Independent Insurance Agents
    2918 Clairmont Avenue
    Birmingham, AL 35205
    (205) 326-4129
    fax (205) 326-3086

Alaska

Alaska Independent Insurance Agents & Brokers
    8300 Briarwood, Suite C
    Anchorage, AK 99518
    (907) 349-2500
    fax (907) 349-1300

Arizona

Independent Insurance Agents & Brokers of Arizona
2828 North 36th Street, Suite C
Phoenix, AZ 85008
(800) 627-3356
(602) 956-1851
fax (602) 468 1392

Arkansas

Independent Insurance Brokers of Arkansas
11225 Hurton Lane, Suite 222
Little Rock, AR 72221
(501) 221-2444
fax (501) 221-0364

California

Insurance Brokers & Agents of the West
101 Market Street, Suite 702
San Francisco, CA 94105
(800) 722-8998 in state only
(415) 957-1212
fax (415) 541-9184

Colorado

Professional Independent Insurance Agents of Colorado, Inc.
1660 South Albion, Suite 518
Denver, CO 80222
(303) 512-0627
fax (303) 512-0575

Connecticut

Independent Insurance Agents of Connecticut Inc.
  30 Jordan Lane
  Wethersfield, CT 06109
  (800) 842-2208 in state only
  (860) 563-1950
  fax (860) 257-9981

Delaware

Independent Insurance Agents of Delaware
  600A North East Front Street
  Milford, DE 19963
  (800) 248-0356 in state only
  (302) 424-4081
  fax (302) 424-4086

District of Columbia

Metropolitan Washington Association of Independent Insurance
    Agents
  127 South Peyton Street
  Alexandria, VA 22314
  (703) 706-5446
  fax (703) 684-6772

Florida

Florida Association of Insurance Agents
  3159 Shamrock South
  Tallahassee, FL 32317
  (850) 893-4155
  fax (850) 668-2852

Georgia

Independent Insurance Agents of Georgia
  3186 Chestnut Drive, Connector
  Doraville, GA 30340
  (800) 878-6487
  (770) 458-0093
  fax (770) 458-8007

Hawaii

Hawaii Independent Insurance Agents Association
  1132 Bishop Street, #1408
  Honolulu, HI 96813
  (808) 531-3125
  fax (808) 531-9995

Idaho

Independent Insurance Agents of Idaho
  595 South 14th
  Boise, ID 83702
  (208) 342-9326
  fax (208) 336-2901

Illinois

Professional Independent Insurance Agents of Illinois
  4630 Wabash
  Springfield, IL 62707
  (800) 628-6436 in state only
  (217) 793-6660
  fax (217) 793-6744

Indiana

Independent Insurance Agents of Indiana
　3435 West 96th Street
　Indianapolis, IN 46268
　(800) 438-4224
　(317) 824-3780
　fax (317) 824-3786

Iowa

Independent Insurance Agents of Iowa
　4000 Westown Parkway
　West Des Moines, IA 50265
　(800) 272-9312 in state only
　(515) 223-6060
　fax (515) 222-0610

Kansas

Kansas Association of Insurance Agents
　815 SW Topeka Avenue
　Topeka, KS 66612
　(800) 229-7048 in state only
　(785) 232-0561
　fax (785) 232-6817

Kentucky

Independent Insurance Agents of Kentucky, Inc.
　10221 Linn Station Road
　Louisville, KY 40223
　(502) 426-0610
　fax (502) 423-8313

Louisiana

Independent Insurance Agents of Louisiana, Inc.
  Suite 2020, One American Place
  Baton Rouge, LA 70825
  (504) 387-5149
  fax (504) 343-1070

Maine

Maine Insurance Agents Association
  432 Western Avenue
  Augusta, ME 04330
  (800) 439-1875
  (207) 623-1875
  fax (207) 626-0275

Maryland

Independent Insurance Agents of Maryland, Inc.
  2408 Peppermill Drive
  Glen Burnie, MD 21061
  (410) 766-0600
  fax (410) 766-0993

Massachusetts

Massachusetts Association of Insurance Agents
  137 Pennsylvania Avenue
  Framingham, MA 01701
  (800) 972-9312 in state only
  (508) 628-5452
  fax (508) 628-5444

Michigan

Michigan Association of Insurance Agents
    1141 Centennial Way
    Lansing, MI 48917
    (517) 323-9473
    fax (517) 323-1629

Minnesota

Minnesota Independent Insurance Agents
    7300 Metro Boulevard, Suite 605
    Edina, MN 55439
    (800) 864-3846
    (612) 835-4180
    fax (612) 835-4774

Mississippi

Independent Insurance Agents of Mississippi
    945 North State Street
    Jackson, MS 39205
    (800) 898-0821
    (601) 354-4595
    fax (601) 354-4622

Missouri

Missouri Association of Insurance Agents
    2701 Industrial Drive
    Jefferson City, MO 65102
    (573) 893-4301
    fax (573) 893-3708

Montana

Independent Insurance Agents of Montana, Inc.
  1200 North Montana Avenue
  Helena, MT 59601
  (406) 442-9555
  fax (406) 442-8263

Nebraska

Independent Insurance Agents of Nebraska
  1023 Lincoln Mall
  Nincoln, NE 68508
  (800) 377-3985
  (402) 476-2951
  fax (402) 476-1586

Nevada

Nevada Independent Insurance Agents
  310 North Stewart Street
  Carson City, NV 89701
  (702) 882-1366
  fax (702) 883-0524

New Hampshire

Independent Insurance Agents of New Hampshire
  125 Airport Road
  Concord, NH 03301
  (800) 559-3373 in state only
  (603) 224-3965
  fax (603) 224-0550

New Jersey

Independent Insurance Agents of New Jersey
  2211 Whitehorse-Mercerville Road
  Trenton, NJ 08619-0230
  (800) 952-6948 in state only
  (609) 587-4333
  fax (609) 587-4515

New Mexico

Independent Insurance Agents of New Mexico, Inc.
  1511 University NE
  Albuquerque, NM 87102
  (800) 621-3978 in state only
  (505) 843-7231
  fax (505) 243-3367

New York

Independent Insurance Agents Association of New York
  109 Twin Oaks Drive
  Syracuse, NY 13206
  (800) 962-7950
  (315) 432-9111
  fax (315) 432-0510

North Carolina

Independent Insurance Agents of North Carolina
  1500 Hillsborough Street
  Raleigh, NC 27605
  (800) 849-6556
  (919) 828-4371
  fax (919) 821-3172

North Dakota

Independent Insurance Agents of North Dakota
  Professional Building
  418 East Rosser Avenue
  Bismarck, ND 58501-4085
  (701) 258-4000
  fax (701) 258-4001

Ohio

The Independent Insurance Agents Association of Ohio, Inc.
  1330 Dublin Road
  Columbus, OH 43215
  (800) 282-4424
  (614) 464-3100
  fax (614) 486-9797

Oklahoma

Oklahoma Association of Insurance Agents
  1000 NW 50th Street
  Oklahoma City, OK 73154
  (800) 324-4426
  (405) 840-4426
  fax (405) 840-4450

Oregon

Insurance Agents Association of Oregon
  2701 NW Vaughn
  Portland, OR 97210
  (503) 274-4000
  fax (503) 274-0062

Pennsylvania

Independent Insurance Agents of Pennsylvania
  2807 North Front Street
  Harrisburg, PA 17110
  (717) 236-4427
  fax (717) 236-6697

Rhode Island

Independent Insurance Agents of Rhode Island
  Warwick, RI 02886
  (401) 732-2400
  fax (401) 732-1708

South Carolina

Independent Insurance Agents of South Carolina
  800 Gracern Road
  Columbia, SC 29210
  (803) 731-9460
  fax (803) 772-6425

South Dakota

Independent Insurance Agents of South Dakota
  222 East Capitol Avenue
  Pierre, SD 57501
  (605) 224-6234
  fax (605) 224-6235

Tennessee

Insurors of Tennessee
  2500 Hillsboro Road
  Nashville, TN 37212
  (615) 385-1898
  fax (615) 385-9303

Texas

Texas Association of Insurance Agents
  1115 San Jaciento, Suite 100
  Austin, TX 78701
  (800) 366-4428
  (512) 476-6281
  fax (512) 469-9512

Utah

The Independent Insurance Agents Association of Utah
  4885 South 900 East, Suite 302
  Salt Lake City, UT 84117
  (801) 269-1200
  fax (801) 269-1265

Vermont

Independent Insurance Agents of Vermont, Inc.
  47½ Court Street
  Montpelier, VT 05601
  (800) 239-4447
  (802) 229-5884
  fax (802) 223-0868

Virginia

Independent Insurance Agents of Virginia, Inc.
  8600 Maryland Drive
  Richmond, VA 23229
  (800) 288-4428
  (804) 747-9300
  fax (804) 747-6557

Washington

Independent Insurance Agents & Brokers of Washington
  15015 Main Street, Suite 205
  Bellevue, WA 98007
  (425) 649-0102
  fax (425) 649-8573

West Virginia

Professional Independent Insurance Agents of West Virginia
179 Summers Street at Lee, Suite 321
Charleston, WV 25301
(800) 274-4298
(304) 342-2440
fax (304) 344-4492

Wisconsin

Independent Insurance Agents of Wisconsin
725 John Nolen Drive
Madison, WI 53713
(800) 362-7441 in state only
(608) 256-4429
fax (608) 256-0170

Wyoming

Association of Wyoming Insurance Agents
3211 Energy Lane, #202
Casper, WY 82602
(307) 235-2101
fax (307) 235-9156

CHAPTER 5

BECOMING CERTIFIED

Secondary education, advanced education, and licensing are components of the insurance educational process. In addition, the insurance industry provides education advancement opportunities through the certification of industry professionals by specific insurance societies. This practice was established to maintain control over the industry above and beyond state licensing regulations. It ensures professionalism among insurance practitioners by stressing knowledge, skills, and codes of ethics.

HISTORY OF CERTIFICATION

Insurance certification had its beginnings in the first collegiate level courses offered to individuals interested in insurance work. Before 1904, few colleges and universities had an inkling as to the exploding insurance field. Therefore, few schools offered courses in insurance. But in 1904, Dr. S. S. Huebner, an instructor at the Wharton School of

Finance and Commerce at the University of Pennsylvania, had the foresight to begin amassing information on the technical and legal aspects of insurance, crafting a collegiate educational program in insurance. From this single university program sprang a host of educational programs for individuals seeking specific knowledge in insurance.

Once the roots of certification were established, several organizations sought to establish stringent guidelines for the flourishing field of insurance—seeking to lead insurance professionals toward high standards of conduct.

In 1909, a number of important associations met in Philadelphia, the birthplace of modern insurance methods, to plan an educational program that would be national in scope. These organizations were the Insurance Society of Philadelphia, the Insurance Society of New York, the Fire Insurance Club of Chicago, the Insurance Institute of Hartford, and the Insurance Library Association of Boston. They sought uniformity in the educational learning of insurance professionals, which in turn would create a uniform insurance system. During this conference, the individual associations banded together to form the Association of Insurance Societies and Institutes of America, the oldest continuously operating national educational program for insurance in the United States.

Once formed, the association set about to create an all-encompassing examination of insurance certification. This written examination, held in June of 1911, drew thirty-four respondents. It was a humble beginning, considering the many thousands of individuals who apply for national examinations today.

Over the years, the association refined testing techniques and took steps toward solidifying testing methods through its permanent incorporation in 1924. With its charter, the association changed its name to the Insurance Institute of America.

Perhaps the most important step toward a systemized level of educational advancement for insurance professionals occurred in 1941. That year several organizations met to take the ideas of the Insurance Institute of America—the very idea of professional insurance education—one step further. The Independent Insurance Agents of America, the National Board of Fire Underwriters, the National Association of Mutual Insurance Agents, the National Association of Insurance Brokers, the Association of Casualty and Surety Executives, and the American Mutual Insurance Alliance met in conference to plan a professional designation program for insurance.

As a result of that meeting, a national college, called the American Institute for Property and Liability Underwriters, was created with the power to issue professional designations in insurance. Thus, the certification of insurance professionals was established, through the origin of the Chartered Property and Casualty Underwriter (CPCU) designation.

THE CHARTERED PROPERTY AND CASUALTY UNDERWRITER (CPCU) DESIGNATION

The Chartered Property and Casualty Underwriter designation reflects a substantial achievement for an insurance professional—a badge of honor, so to speak. The designation is awarded to individuals who pass a series of complex tests regarding insurance law and procedures. It is so worthwhile that every year a number of people in professions outside the insurance industry take the courses and examination in order to obtain a proficiency in insurance matters. In truth, the knowledge of the insurance industry and its workings obtained from CPCU courses can benefit a number of professions in the business sector, from accountancy to financial analysis. Therefore, the CPCU examinations are worthwhile to all business professionals.

Topics in CPCU courses cover a wide range of areas, including insurance, risk management, and general business topics. Insurance and risk management principles are applied to the treatment of personal and commercial losses. In addition, insurance policy examples are examined in detail.

Since insurance professionals operate within a business setting, the CPCU curriculum includes courses on economics, accounting, management, and finance in order to prepare the professional for the possibility of career advancement. The courses also emphasize topics of importance to the field of insurance and risk management.

CPCU courses (and subsequent examinations) are recommended for experienced insurance professionals who have a strong knowledge of basic practices, including risk managers, sales professionals, safety professionals, accountants, professors of insurance, attorneys, and other individuals who are in careers requiring an understanding of insurance functions.

These courses serve to expand upon an individual's existing knowledge of the insurance field, using the professional's past experiences as a foundation for advanced theories and practices. For this reason, insurance professionals who consider taking the examination in the future are best advised to continue amassing knowledge while in the field. Clearly, insurance is not a field where one can rest on one's laurels. In truth, the road to certification is paved with experience, dedication, and insight toward advancement.

The CPCU courses are offered in sequences. The best sequence for an individual to take depends on the amount and type of experiences he or she has had in the workplace. Individuals from an insurance agency or company background should first take courses that build on past experiences. For instance, those who work in life insurance should seek out the course that best applies to life insurance situations. Thus, individuals build on successes, using prior knowledge to ease into course work. Easing into education this way works best for individuals who have been away from educational pursuits for some time, building confidence for their return to the rigors of academics.

Following are descriptions of the ten courses needed to prepare for the ten CPCU examinations:

Course One—Principles of Risk Management and Insurance. This course describes the risk management framework for the insurance field, the insurance environment, and various principles of insurance contract analysis.

Course Two—Personal Risk Management and Insurance. This course relates risk management concepts to individual and family risk exposures. Case studies used in this course illustrate the role of property and liability insurance, life and health insurance, social insurance, employee benefits, retirement planning, and coordinated insurance buying in personal risk management.

Course Three—Commercial Property Risk Management and Insurance. This course begins with an analysis and measurement of commercial loss exposures. The course then examines the major commercial policies and forms, including fire and allied lines, business interruption, ocean and inland marine, crime, and combination policies. Related risk management control and financing techniques are also discussed within the context of the course.

Course Four—Commercial Liability Risk Management and Insurance. This course analyzes the major sources of liability loss exposures. Then the course examines the insurance coverages designed to meet those exposures. Premises and operations, products and completed operations, contractual and protective liability, employers' liability and workers' compensation, automobile liability, and professional liability are discussed within the course's framework. Surety bonds are also covered in the course.

Course Five—Insurance Company Operations. This course examines insurance marketing, underwriting, reinsurance, rate making, claims adjustment, loss control activities, and other operations.

Course Six—The Legal Environment of Insurance. This course is based on general business law, with an emphasis on the areas of tort, contract, and agency law. The course also emphasizes the application of business law to insurance operations and situations.

Course Seven—Management. This course covers management principles and problems. The course also offers an introduction to insurance management information systems.

Course Eight—Accounting and Finance. This course provides a generalized college-level treatment of basic accounting and finance principles. After the student has mastered these basic principles, the course moves on to cover how these principles relate to property and liability insurance accounting and finance operations.

Course Nine—Economics. This course covers general economic principles at both the macro and micro levels.

Course Ten—Insurance Issues and Professional Ethics. This course analyzes significant problems and issues that affect the insurance industry. The course also focuses on professional ethics in general and the American Institute Code of Professional Ethics in particular. This code of ethics, adopted by the American Institute for Property and Liability Underwriters for individuals who are designated CPCUs, binds the CPCU to a systemized number of moral codes regarding conduct. These codes are referred to as a professional charge. The professional charge reads as follows:

> In all my business dealings and activities, I agree to abide by the following rules of professional conduct: I shall strive at all times to ascertain and understand the needs of those whom I serve and act as if their interests were my own; and I shall do all in my power to maintain and uphold a standard of honor and integrity that will reflect credit on the business in which I am engaged.

Clearly, certification stands for something more than pure educational advancement. It also stands for higher principles—a way of life. Through the rigorous course work and examinations, certification seeks to create the most moral and intelligent professional to serve the public.

Beyond certification as a Chartered Property and Casualty Underwriter, an individual can become certified in a number of other capacities, leading up to certification as a CPCU. Following are brief descriptions of the various designations:

ASSOCIATE IN CLAIMS (AIC)

The AIC designation is appropriate for experienced insurance adjusters, claims personnel, and those individuals who deal with property losses and liability claims. The program leading to certification as an Associate in Claims outlines principal concepts that involve insurance claims processes and practices, the writing of claims reports, and the reviewing of claim files. The program also includes in-depth discussions of medical terminology and practices, useful information for adjusters working with medical liability cases.

ASSOCIATE IN MANAGEMENT (AIM)

This form of certification is designed for middle management professionals, as well as those seeking middle management positions. Programs leading to this designation concentrate on the strengths and weaknesses of existing management practices, human behavior, and systematic decision-making processes. Courses also outline leadership roles in management.

ASSOCIATE IN RISK MANAGEMENT (ARM)

The ARM certification can be of significant value to those responsible for controlling and financing risks of losses suffered by their own company. The designation is also of value to producers who are interested in providing risk management counseling for their individual clients. In addition, underwriters can use the course offered leading to this designation to sharpen their risk selection.

Programs designed for this designation offer techniques for the identification and evaluation of loss exposures, as well as the analysis of risk control. Financing techniques for exposures, selection of risk management alternatives, and the implementation of risk control and risk financing techniques are also discussed within the context of ARM courses.

ASSOCIATE IN UNDERWRITING (AU)

Designed for individuals experienced in underwriting and business placement, this form of certification appeals especially to agency and company underwriters and field representatives. Courses are offered leading to this designation, highlighting principles of underwriting for property and liability insurance, personal lines insurance, and commercial liability underwriting.

ASSOCIATE IN LOSS CONTROL MANAGEMENT (ALCM)

This form of certification is designed for individuals who deal with the selection, design, and implementation of loss control programs. Courses leading to this designation concentrate on the analysis of fundamental principles used in controlling losses to people and property. Courses also apply these principles to various case situations.

ASSOCIATE IN PREMIUM AUDITING (APA)

The APA certification is designed for insurance premium auditors who wish to increase their professional knowledge of property and liability insurance contracts, auditing procedures appropriate to various situations, principles of insurance, insurance accounting, and the premium auditor's relationship with other insurance functions.

ASSOCIATE IN RESEARCH AND PLANNING (ARP)

Courses leading to this designation provide an educational foundation for insurance personnel working in research, planning, and related decision support functions. Courses then provide individuals with the opportunity to learn the most up-to-date research and planning methods. In addition, such courses cover basic insurance principles.

ASSOCIATE IN INSURANCE ACCOUNTING AND FINANCE (AIAF)

Geared toward individuals with a professional knowledge of accounting procedures, courses leading to this designation concentrate on the financial operations of insurance entities, providing individuals with the opportunity to master statutory accounting principles, reporting procedures, and financial management concepts.

All courses for these designations are available through the Insurance Institute of America. In addition to the educational aspects of certification provided by these courses, each designation allows the individual to waive certain requirements needed for course work toward certification as a CPCU. Thus, individuals can use prior certification as a means of advancement.

Those interested in certification courses are urged to contact the institute at the following address:

Insurance Institute of America
  720 Providence Road
  Malvern, PA 19355
  (610) 644–2100

THE CHARTERED LIFE UNDERWRITER (CLU) DESIGNATION

In addition to property and casualty designations, the insurance field offers certification for life insurance practitioners.

Like the CPCU designation, the Chartered Life Underwriter (CLU) designation is thought of as the pinnacle of systemized insurance education. Individuals seeking the distinction of certification as a Chartered Life Underwriter must pass ten individual examinations, covering such topics as the law and life insurance, estate planning, business planning, pension plans, group and social insurance, accounting principles, and finance theories.

Like the CPCU examinations, the courses offered leading to the CLU designation build on existing knowledge, using it as a framework for expanded study. Again, the individual who is seriously considering career advancement through certification as a Chartered Life Underwriter would be wise to amass knowledge while working in the insurance field. Then the road to certification would be easier.

Courses leading to CLU certification are available from the American College in Bryn Mawr, Pennsylvania. Interested persons may write the college at the following address:

American College
  Bryn Mawr, PA 19010

CHAPTER 6

INSURANCE ASSOCIATIONS

Professional associations can sometimes be nothing more than organizations for individuals with like-minded interests to meet and discuss topics of the day. Within the insurance industry, however, professional associations play an important role.

These organizations serve to inform their charter members about current trends within the field, such as changing legislation, new business procedures, and economic developments. Additionally, most professional associations provide seminars and forums to further educate members about the ever-changing field of insurance. The organizations also provide valuable networking contacts—networking being that informal business skill involving meeting people in the field for future professional contact.

Professional organizations can be incredibly helpful to individuals considering careers in the insurance industry. For one, an organization can serve as a networking connection between the interested individual and an insurance company with regard to internship possibilities. Because many insurance companies and agencies seek employees who already have knowledge of the insurance business, internships may provide an individual with a fundamental understanding of the day-to-day workings of an agency or company. A successful internship with an insurance company or agency also provides the individual with a ready source of professional references—something that is hard to obtain at a university or college. A graduating student with an internship listed on a resume sends out a subtle signal to a prospective employer, one that shows an interviewer that the student is truly interested in the field. Most important, an internship may provide an individual with insight about the insurance profession and may help the student make career decisions based on actual, not textbook, experience.

Beyond internship possibilities, professional associations may provide individuals with interview sources; thus one may talk directly with people in insurance about career choices. Often, the "voice of experience" can help an individual make the right decisions involving career directions.

Following is a list of professional insurance organizations nationwide, with brief descriptions as to individual activities and membership. Contact associations in your area to get a better understanding of the types of career opportunities available in your region. Many associations have chapter offices in other cities or would know of insurance companies and agencies to contact in other cities.

Alliance of American Insurers
  3205 Highland Parkway, Suite 800
  Downers Grove, IL 60515
  (630) 724-2100

This association of property and casualty companies was founded in 1922 and currently has more than 260 members. The association publishes the quarterly *Journal of American Insurance.*

Allnations
   One Nationwide Plaza
   Columbus, OH 43215
   (614) 249-7002

Founded in 1966, this association provides assistance to developing cooperative insurance companies—companies that unite to provide coverage to any type of risk. When a loss occurs, each company then provides a portion of a claim, spreading risk to financially assist each other in claims coverage.

American Academy of Actuaries
   1100 17th Street, NW, 7th Floor
   Washington, DC 20036
   (202) 223-8196

This association benefits the actuary, the individual who applies mathematical probabilities to the design of insurance coverage. The association promotes educational advancement for actuaries, as well as education of the public on actuarial matters. In addition, the organization seeks to maintain high levels of competence for all members, acting as an accreditation body for actuaries. The organization was formed from four distinct associations, including the Fraternal Actuarial Association, the Conference of Actuaries in Public Practice, the Casualty Actuarial Society, and the Society of Actuaries.

The association provides a speakers bureau of professionals who can lecture before interested groups.

American Association of Dental Consultants
  P.O. Box 3345
  Lawrence, KS 66046
  (785) 749-2727

This association, founded in 1977, was formed by dental insurance consultants to increase awareness in dental insurance plans. The association has a certification program for dental insurance consultants and also holds workshops for educational advancement.

American Association of Insurance Services
  1035 South York Road
  Bensenville, IL 60106
  (630) 595-3225

This association compiles statistics and creates rates for fire, casualty, multiple line, and inland marine insurance. The association also provides rules that are filed with state insurance departments. The association publishes *Viewpoint,* a bimonthly publication.

American Association of Managing General Agents
  9140 Ward Parkway
  Kansas City, MO 64114
  (816) 444-3500

Founded in 1926, this association provides an educational forum for managing general agents of insurance companies. The association also compiles statistics and provides a speakers bureau for interested groups. The association publishes a monthly newsletter, which provides information on the role of managing general agents.

American Cargo War Risk Reinsurance Exchange
   14 Wall Street
   New York, NY 10005
   (212) 233-3180

Founded in 1939, this organization was created to spread insurance risks for ocean cargo during wartime. Now, the organization's members include insurance companies in the specialized field of ocean marine insurance.

American Council of Life Insurance
   1001 Pennsylvania Avenue NW
   Washington, DC 20004
   (202) 624-2000

Members of the American Council of Life Insurance include legal reserve life insurance companies. The council represents the life insurance business in government and conducts research programs through the compilation of statistics. The council also operates educational and consumer services. In addition, the council has a ten thousand–volume library of insurance books and publications and publishes a host of material, including an annual *Life Insurance Fact Book,* brochures, and statistics.

American Hull Insurance Syndicate
   14 Wall Street
   New York, NY 10005
   (212) 233-0300

This association acts as a syndicate for the insurance of oceangoing and Great Lakes ships and foreign hulls. The association also acts as a syndicate for the writing of insurance on shipbuilders' risks. The association is designed to assist the development of the American Merchant Marine and the foreign trade and commerce of the United States, offering protection to maritime tradespeople.

American Institute for CPCU
  720 Providence Road
  Malvern, PA 19355
  (215) 644-2100

Established in 1942, the institute determines the qualifications for professional certification of insurance personnel. The institute also works with universities and colleges with regard to educational standards. Most important, the institute holds examinations and awards certification for the designation of Chartered Property Casualty Underwriter (CPCU), an industry standard. The institute also maintains a vast library of resources on insurance, business, and finance. As part of its services, the institute publishes CPCU course guides and textbooks for insurance professionals.

American Institute of Marine Underwriters
  14 Wall Street
  New York, NY 10005
  (212) 233-0550

Founded in 1898, this association of marine insurance companies offers training and educational seminars on marine insurance, as well as the analysis of international agreements affecting marine insurance. The association publishes a daily bulletin.

American Insurance Association
  1130 Connecticut Avenue, NW, Suite 1000
  Washington, DC 20036
  (202) 828-7100

This association represents companies that provide property and liability insurance. The association promotes the standing of members through activities, including industry accounting procedures, catastrophe procedures, automobile insurance reform, rating laws, property insurance programs for highway safety, fire prevention, and workers' compensation law reforms. The association also publishes informational bulletins on fire prevention, industrial safety rules, and various laws.

American Insurers Highway Safety Alliance
  1501 Woodfield Road, Suite 400 W
  Schaumburg, IL 60173
  (708) 330-8500

Founded in 1920, this association of automobile insurance companies offers programs on accident prevention. The association also publishes a variety of newsletters on traffic safety.

American Nuclear Insurers
  29 South Main Street
  West Hartford, CT 06107-2430
  (860) 561-3433

Established in 1974, this association consists of insurance companies formed to provide property and liability insurance protection for the nuclear energy industry.

American Society of Chartered Life Underwriters
  270 Bryn Mawr Avenue
  Bryn Mawr, PA 19010
  (610) 526-2500

This association, founded in 1927, is a professional society of insurance agents, accountants, attorneys, and trust officers who hold professional designations as Chartered Life Underwriter (CLU) or Chartered Financial Consultant (ChFC). The society holds graduate level educational programs and seminars for members. The society also publishes a variety of publications regarding insurance.

Associated Risk Managers International
  816 Congress Avenue
  Austin, TX 78701
  (512) 479-6886

This association was formed for independent insurance agencies that provide property and casualty insurance, risk management services, and life and health insurance programs. The association develops and markets specialized insurance and risk management services for trade associations, professional groups, and industry organizations. The association also holds education seminars, maintains a library on insurance and risk management related matters, compiles statistics, and operates a speakers bureau for interested groups.

Association for Advanced Life Underwriting
  1922 F Street NW
  Washington, DC 20006
  (202) 331-6081

Founded in 1957, the association caters to advanced life underwriters who specialize in estate analysis, business insurance, pension planning, and employee benefit plans.

Association of Average Adjusters of the United States
  79 Palmer Drive
  Livingston, NJ 07039-1314
  (973) 597-0824

This association for marine insurance adjusters maintains an extensive library on marine insurance and topics pertinent to this specialized field.

Association of Canadian Insurers
  2 Sheppard Avenue East, Suite 800
  Toronto, Ontario M2N 5Y7
  (416) 733-8722

As a trade organization for Canadian owned insurers, this organization plays a public relations role for member companies. It also provides a variety of member services.

Canadian Life and Health Insurance Association
  1 Queen Street East, Suite 1700
  Toronto, Ontario M5C 2X9
  (416) 777-2221

This large association serves insurers throughout Canada. It promotes good business practices and serves the needs of insurance companies as well as those of consumers and businesses that deal with insurance companies.

Captive Insurance Companies Association
  4248 Park Glen Road
  Minneapolis, MN 55416
  (401) 946-2310

This association of insurance companies was originally formed to provide coverage for sponsor organizations such as manufacturers and retailers. The association provides information to firms trying to solve corporate insurance dilemmas.

Casualty Actuarial Society
  1100 North Glebe Road, Suite 600
  Arlington, VA 22201
  (703) 276-3100

This professional society of insurance actuaries promotes actuarial and statistical sciences in the fields of casualty, fire, and social insurance. The association also promotes education in the actuarial sciences and requires all members to pass educational examinations.

Conference of Casualty Insurance Companies
  3601 Vincennes Road
  Indianapolis, IN 46268
  (317) 872-4061

Founded in 1930, this association for casualty insurance companies promotes educational programs for executives of member firms. The association also conducts seminars on problems of individual departments of casualty companies, such as fire, inland marine, underwriting, claims, and data processing.

Conference of Consulting Actuaries
1110 West Lake Cook Road
Buffalo Grove, IL 60089-1968
(847) 419-9090

A conference for full-time consulting or governmental actuaries, the association monitors professional conduct and educational aspects of its members.

Consumer Credit Insurance Association
542 South Dearborn, #400
Chicago, IL 60605
(312) 939-2242

This association was established for insurance companies that underwrite consumer credit insurance in the areas of life, accident, health, and property insurance. The association also publishes a monthly newsletter that outlines topics of interest in the field of consumer credit insurance.

Crop Insurance Research Bureau
9200 Indian Creek Parkway, Suite 220
Overland Park, KS 66210
(913) 338-0470

Established in 1964, this association serves crop insurance companies and organizations related to the crop insurance industry, promoting accuracy in hail loss settlements. The association also promotes educational efforts of its members through training of crop adjusters and other crop insurance professionals. In addition, the organization provides funding for agricultural university research on crops and crop adjusting procedures, as well as educational seminars and workshops.

Direct Marketing Insurance Council
c/o Direct Marketing Association
Six East 43rd Street
New York, NY 10017
(212) 689-4977

Members of this association include direct response marketing divisions of insurance companies. The association provides educational seminars and publishes several newsletters on direct marketing in insurance.

Eastern Claims Conference
c/o John Healy
111 John Street
New York, NY 10038
(212) 732-5343

The conference provides educational seminars to disability examiners, including life, health, and group claim insurance professionals. The educational seminars are designed for those professionals who review medical and disability claims. The conference maintains a speakers bureau and several informational publications.

Factory Mutual System
1151 Boston-Providence Turnpike
Norwood, MA 02062
(617) 762-4300

This organization was established for mutual insurance companies insuring industrial and commercial properties in the United States and Canada. It provides consultations, inspections, fire prevention services, and research capabilities to its members.

Foreign Credit Insurance Association
  40 Rector Street, 11th Floor
  New York, NY 10006
  (212) 306-5000

This organization of marine, property, and casualty insurance companies enables U.S. exporters to compete on equal terms with exporters in other countries through the use of coverage for overseas products sales. The association also encourages United States service industries to expand their services into foreign countries.

Fraternal Field Managers' Association
  4321 North Ballard Road
  Appleton, WI 54919
  (920) 734-5721

Founded in 1935, this association of sales managers for fraternal life insurance societies sponsors a designation of Fraternal Insurance Counselor (FIC) for members meeting educational and production requirements.

General Agents and Managers Conference of the National
    Association of Underwriters
  1922 F Street NW
  Washington, DC 20006
  (202) 331-6088

This association is geared toward life insurance general agents, life insurance managers, assistant agency heads, home office officials, and other insurance professionals who are interested in life insurance field management. The association strives to improve the quality of management, primarily through educational programs, code of ethics practices, and research programs. The association also provides training in management for insurance professionals.

Health Insurance Association of America
   555 13th Street NW
   Washington, DC 20004
   (202) 824-1600

This association of accident and health insurance firms strives to promote the development of voluntary insurance against loss of income resulting from sickness or accident; it does so through educational forums and research programs.

Highway Loss Data Institute
   1005 North Glebe Road, Suite 1800
   Arlington, VA 22201
   (703) 247-1600

Established as an association for motor vehicle property and casualty companies, the institute gathers, processes, and provides the public with information and insurance data regarding human and economic losses resulting from highway crashes.

Independent Insurance Agents of America
   127 South Peyton Street
   Alexandria, VA 22314
   (703) 683-4422

Founded in 1896, this association represents more than three hundred thousand agents and their employees located throughout the United States. Organized for insurance sales agencies handling fire and casualty insurance, the Independent Insurance Agents of America provides technical courses for members and publishes handbooks and pamphlets on subjects pertaining to fire and casualty insurance.

Inland Marine Underwriters Association
111 Broadway, 15th Floor
New York, NY 10006
(212) 233-7958

This association of insurance companies transacting inland marine insurance provides a forum for members on problems within the industry. The association also makes legislative recommendations with regard to inland marine insurance regulations and provides specialized education courses for members.

Institute of Home Office Underwriters
American Family Life Insurance Company
6000 American Parkway
Madison, WI 53783
(608) 249-0100

Established in 1937, this association of corporate-sponsored home office life insurance underwriters works to increase awareness and underwriting knowledge of its members through specialized educational programs and seminars. The association also prepares examinations for member fellowship in the Academy of Life Underwriting and conducts studies on phases of underwriting.

Insurance Accounting and Systems Association
P.O. Box 51340
Durham, NC 27717
(919) 489-0991

This association provides a forum for accountants, actuarial consultants, management consultants, statisticians, and statistical organizations. The association also provides members with research in the field of insurance.

Insurance Bureau of Canada
181 University Avenue, 13th Floor
Toronto, Ontario M5H 3M7
(416) 362-2031

This national trade association has represented insurance companies doing business in Canada since 1964. It promotes cooperation among insurers, government, businesses, and others.

Insurance Information Institute
110 William Street
New York, NY 10038
(212) 669-9200

This association of property and liability insurance companies provides information and educational programs to the media, educational institutions, trade associations, governmental agencies, businesses, and the public on insurance matters and issues. The association also sponsors seminars and briefings on research and economic topics. In addition, the Insurance Information Institute maintains a library on insurance topics and operates a consumer hot line.

Insurance Institute of America
    720 Providence Road
    Malvern, PA 19355
    (610) 644-2100

The Insurance Institute of America sponsors educational programs for property and liability insurance personnel and conducts examinations for member certification. The association also maintains a vast library of volumes pertaining to insurance topics and related matters, such as finances and economics.

Insurance Institute of Canada
    18 King Street East, 6th Floor
    Toronto, Ontario M5C 1C4
    (416) 362-8586

The Insurance Institute provide educational services for the Canadian property/casualty insurance industry. It maintains uniform educational standards and manages a certification process for insurance professionals.

Insurance Marketing Communications Association
    9710 North 80th Place
    Scottsdale, AZ 85258
    (602) 443-8860

Founded in 1923, this association serves advertising, marketing, sales promotions, and public relations executives of insurance companies.

Insurance Premium Finance Association
2890 Niagra Falls
Amherst, NY 14226
(716) 695-8757

Founded in 1961, this association caters to firms licensed by the state of New York to finance automobile and other liability insurance premiums on an installment basis.

Insurance Services Office
7 World Trade Center
New York, NY 10048
(212) 898-5525

This association for property and liability insurance companies provides insurers with statistical, actuarial, policy, and other related services, such as fire protection gradings for municipalities and fire insurance surveys for specific properties. The Insurance Services Office also acts as an advisory organization on insurance matters and issues. The association publishes a variety of materials, including rate handbooks and policy statements.

Insurance Society of New York
c/o The College of Insurance
One Insurance Plaza
101 Murray Street
New York, NY 10007
(212) 815-9237

The Insurance Society of New York is the parent company of the College of Insurance, a fully accredited educational institution offering M.B.A., B.B.A, B.S., and A.O.S.

degrees. The association maintains a vast library of insurance materials, including books, pamphlets, and historical documents. The association also sponsors periodic lectures on insurance issues.

International Claim Association
  1255 23rd Street NW
  Washington, DC 20037-1174
  (202) 452-0143

Founded in 1909, this association caters to claims executives and administrators of insurance companies writing life, health, or accident insurance.

Intersure
  c/o Alvin Singer
  836 Palisade Avenue
  P.O. Box 16
  Teaneck, NJ 07666
  (201) 692-1700

Intersure was established for commercial lines insurance agencies that have a volume of one million dollars annually and have a separate life department. This association promotes an exchange of experience and techniques among members. The association achieves its goals through a combination of functions, including risk evaluation and claims.

IRM
  4401 Barclay Downs Drive
  Charlotte, NC 28209
  (704) 551-3000

Formerly called Improved Risk Mutuals, this association for mutual and stock insurance companies reinsures large property risks for its member companies, their affiliates, and subsidiaries.

Life Insurers Conference
  2300 Windy Ridge Parkway
  Atlanta, GA 30339
  (770) 933-9954

Founded in 1910, this association serves multiple line and combination life insurance companies writing life, accident, and sickness insurance.

Life Office Management Association
  2300 Windy Ridge Parkway
  Atlanta, GA 30339
  (770) 951-1770

Established for life insurance companies, this association provides research, information, and educational activities in areas of operations and systems, human resources, and financial planning and control. The association administers the FLMI Insurance Education Program, which awards the designation Fellow, Life Management Institute (FLMI) to life insurance company employees who complete a nine-examination program. The association also maintains a library of research materials relating to company operations.

LIMRA International
  Box 208
  Hartford, CT 06141
  (860) 688-3358

Founded in 1945, this association conducts market, economic, financial, and human resources research. The association also monitors industry distribution systems and product and service developments. In addition, the association provides executive and field management development schools and seminars for the insurance industry. The association maintains a library on life insurance marketing and industrial psychology.

Loss Executives Association
   c/o Industrial Risk Insurers
   85 Woodland Street
   Hartford, CT 06102
   (860) 953-2211

Founded in 1921, this association was established for loss executives of insurance companies and serves as a liaison between members and independent adjusters.

Mass Marketing Insurance Institute
   2841 Main
   Kansas City, MO 64108

This association of independent brokers, carriers, and companies active in mass marketing insurance serves to provide pertinent information on insurance issues to its members.

Million Dollar Round Table
   325 West Touhy
   Park Ridge, IL 60068
   (847) 692-6378

Founded in 1927, this association of life insurance agents who sell a predescribed amount of insurance each calendar year conducts several surveys on life insurance.

Mortgage Insurance Companies of America
727 15th Street NW
Washington, DC 20005
(202) 393-5566

This association of United States and Canadian mortgage insurance companies provides representation before Congress as well as federal and state regulatory agencies that review housing-related legislation. It also maintains a forum for discussion of industry-wide standards. In addition, the association compiles statistics on topics related to mortgage insurance.

Mutual Atomic Energy Liability Underwriters
330 North Wabash
Chicago, IL 60611
(312) 467-0003

This underwriting syndicate of four mutual casualty insurance companies writes nuclear energy liability policies in the ever-expanding field of nuclear energy.

National Association of Casualty and Surety Agents
6931 Arlington Road, Suite 308
Bethesda, MD 20814
(301) 986-4166

Founded in 1913, this association caters to agents handling fire, casualty, and surety insurance.

National Association of Casualty and Surety Executives
  1130 Connecticut Avenue NW, Suite 1000
  Washington, DC 20036
  (202) 828-7104

Founded in 1891, the National Association of Casualty and Surety Executives is a professional society for insurance executives and was formed by the merger of the International Association of Casualty and Surety Underwriters and the Board of Casualty and Surety Underwriters.

National Association of Crop Insurance Agents
  6701 Highway 10
  Ramsey, MN 55303
  (612) 427-3770

The association was established for service agents and agencies selling Federal All-Risk Crop Insurance to plant farmers. It provides information about insurance coverage on damages resulting from drought, floods, tornadoes, and other crop disasters.

National Association of Fire Investigators
  P.O. Box 957257
  Hoffman Estates, IL 60195
  (312) 427-6320

This association of fire investigators, insurance adjusters, firefighters, attorneys, and members of related professions was established to increase knowledge and improve the skills of persons engaged in the investigation of fires, explosions, and arson. The association also presents awards to members and compiles statistics on fires, fire fatalities, and fire losses. In addition, the association maintains a library on fire-related insurance issues.

National Association of Fraternal Insurance Counsellors
    P.O. Box 357
    Sheboygan, WI 53082
    (929) 458-1996

This professional organization of sales personnel for fraternal benefit life insurance societies promotes and educates the sales force in fraternal life insurance.

National Association of Health Underwriters
    2000 North 14th Street, Suite 450
    Arlington, VA 22201
    (703) 276-0220

Founded in 1930, this association was formed for insurance agencies and individuals engaged in the promotion, sale, and administration of disability income and health insurance. It sponsors advanced health insurance underwriting seminars at universities, as well as other seminars on underwriting topics. The association also testifies before federal and state committees on health insurance legislation. In addition, the association grants certification to qualified underwriters.

National Association of Independent Insurance Adjusters
    300 West Washington, Suite 805
    Chicago, IL 60606
    (312) 853-0808

This association caters to claims adjusters and firms operating independently on a fee basis for all insurance companies. It is the originator of an adjusters educational program administered by the Insurance Institute of America.

National Association of Independent Insurers
  2600 River Road
  Des Plaines, IL 60018
  (847) 297-7800

Established in 1945, this association of independent property and liability insurance companies compiles and develops statistics through its Independent Statistical Service. The association also develops simplified statistical plans and provides advisory services to members. In addition, the association maintains a library on the law and related subjects.

National Association of Independent Life Brokerage Agencies
  8201 Greensboro Drive
  McLean, VA 22102
  (703) 610-9020

The National Association of Independent Life Brokerage Agencies is comprised of licensed independent life brokerage agencies that represent at least three insurance companies but are not controlled or owned by an underwriting company. The association seeks to further educational plans of members through the application of technological and systems advancements. The association also sponsors research in computer applications to the field, promotion, advertising, and potential profit centers. In addition, the association also promotes legislation and regulations that are beneficial to its members and the field in general.

National Association of Insurance Brokers
  1300 I Street NW
  Washington DC 20005
  (202) 628-6700

Founded in 1934, the National Association of Insurance Brokers caters to sole proprietors, partnerships, and corporations acting as insurance brokers, primarily in the areas of commercial, industrial and institutional risks, and related insurance. The association serves legislative functions for its members, seeking to shape the regulatory environment for the industry.

National Association of Insurance Women—International
  P.O. Box 4410
  1847 East 15th
  Tulsa, OK 74159
  (918) 744-5195

This association for women in the insurance business sponsors educational programs for members and awards a designation of Certified Professional Insurance Woman to those members who pass one of several sets of national examinations.

National Association of Life Companies
  1455 Pennsylvania Avenue NW, Suite 1250
  Washington, DC 20004
  (202) 783-6252

This association of life and health insurance companies conducts specialized education for members and keeps members informed on current legislative matters.

National Association of Life Underwriters
    1922 F Street NW
    Washington, DC 20006
    (202) 331-6000

Founded in 1890, this federation of state and local associations represents more than 128,000 life insurance agents, general agents, and managers. Associate members of the association include home office officials of life companies, life insurance instructors, and journalists. The association seeks to support and maintain the principles of legal reserve life and health insurance while promoting high ethical standards. The association also sponsors public service programs and an educational series.

National Association of Mutual Insurance Companies
    3601 Vincennes Road
    Indianapolis, IN 46268-0700
    (317) 875-5250

Founded in 1895, this association of mutual fire and casualty insurance companies gathers, compiles, and analyzes information on insurance matters and the reduction of losses. The association also conducts regional workshops and seminars. In addition, the association distributes several publications pertaining to the insurance field.

National Association of Public Insurance Adjusters
  300 Water Street, Suite 400
  Baltimore, MD 21202
  (410) 539-4141

This professional society sponsors seminars and professional education programs for members. In addition, the National Association of Public Insurance Adjusters publishes a variety of materials, including bulletins, brochures, and charts.

National Association of Surety Bond Producers
  5225 Wisconsin Avenue NW, Suite 600
  Washington, DC 20015
  (202) 686-3700

Founded in 1942, this association of insurance agents and brokers who write surety bonds provides a forum on pertinent issues for members. The association also publishes a journal on the surety field.

National Committee on Property Insurance
  10 Winthrop Square
  Boston, MA 02110
  (617) 423-4620

The committee serves as a format network for insurance personnel, providing assistance to insurance companies that write insurance coverage in distressed insurance markets. The committee also serves as a liaison for property and casualty insurers with the government, other organizations, and the public. In addition, the committee maintains the

Property Insurance Plans Service Office to assist property and casualty insurance plans in their operations. The committee also conducts research pertinent to the field.

National Council on Compensation Insurance
750 Park of Commerce Drive
Boca Raton, FL 33487
(800) 622-4123

Founded in 1919, this association for insurance companies that write workers' compensation insurance conducts rate making, research, and statistical programs.

National Council of Self-Insurers
Ten South Riverside Plaza, Suite 1530
Chicago, IL 60606
(312) 454-5110

This council of state associations and individual companies concerned with self-insurance under the workers' compensation laws promotes and protects the interests of self-insurers in legislative matters. The council uses its resources to assist and advise self-insurers with aspects of insurance implementation.

National Crop Insurance Services
7201 West 129th Street, Suite 200
Overland Park, KS 66213
(913) 685-2767

Founded in 1989 as a merger of two other crop insurance associations, this is an association of property insurance companies writing hail and collateral insurance for crop growers. The association develops procedures and educational training for crop insurance adjusters. It also sponsors crop damage research projects at various universities.

National Federation of Grange Mutual Insurance Companies
   769 Hebron Avenue, Box 6517
   Glastonbury, CT 06033-6517
   (860) 633-4678

The National Federation of Grange Mutual Insurance Companies provides reinsurance to promote Grange mutual insurance to members.

National Insurance Association
   P.O. Box 53230
   Chicago, IL 60053
   (773) 924-3308

Founded in 1921, the National Insurance Association conducts the educational Institute in Agency Management and the Institute in Home Office Operations. The association also sponsors National Insurance Week.

National Society of Insurance Premium Auditors
   5818 Reeds Road
   Mission, KS 66202
   (913) 262-0163

This association caters to insurance company employees who are engaged in field, administrative, or support service policy auditing to determine insurance premiums. The association acts as a forum for the exchange of new ideas in auditing procedures, as well as technical innovations and developments. The association also develops uniform standards for auditing, promotes and conducts research, and holds educational seminars. In conjunction with the Insurance Institute of America, the association sponsors technical education programs leading to member certification as Associate in Premium Auditing. The association maintains a library of insurance materials, including pamphlets, textbooks, and videotapes.

Organized Flying Adjusters
  5940 Basil Street NE
  Salem, OR 97301
  (503) 585-1318

This association of aircraft insurance adjusters promotes high standards in the processing of insurance claims and seeks to objectively investigate the causes of aviation accidents while promoting air safety. The association also conducts seminars for attorneys, company claims personnel, and manufacturers' representatives on crash investigations and the legal implications involved in aircraft investigations.

Professional Insurance Agents
  400 North Washington Street
  Alexandria, VA 22314
  (703) 836-9340

Founded in 1931, this association of independent property and casualty agents sponsors educational programs and seminars annually on aspects of property and casualty insurance. The association also maintains a legislative division in the nation's capital to assist members with pending legislation vital to their interests. In addition, the association compiles statistics, offers consultation and evaluation services, and conducts research. The association maintains a vast library on a range of insurance issues.

Professional Insurance Marketing Association
  4733 Bethesda Avenue, Suite 330
  Bethesda, MD 20814
  (301) 951-1260

The Professional Insurance Marketing Association was established for insurance companies and agencies. It promotes the mass marketing of insurance services while encouraging favorable regulations and legislation for the entire industry. The association establishes codes of ethics for its members and holds seminars to further member education.

Property Loss Research Bureau
  3025 Highland Parkway
  Downers Grove, IL 60515
  (847) 330-8650

The bureau, sponsored by mutual and stock insurance companies, holds annual conferences for loss managers of insurance companies.

Reinsurance Association of America
  1301 Pennsylvania Avenue NW, Suite 900
  Washington, DC 20004
  (202) 638-3690

This association of companies that write property and casualty reinsurance promotes the interests of the reinsurance industry through legislative actions before Congress and state regulatory agencies and commissions. The association also furthers the interests of the industry through the acquisition and dissemination of information and statistics regarding political developments, economic conditions, and technological advancements.

Risk and Insurance Management Society
655 Third Avenue
New York, NY 10017
(212) 286-9292

Established for corporate risk and insurance managers, this association provides a forum for members to interchange ideas about the insurance field. The association also sponsors educational seminars, conducts research, and compiles statistics on matters pertinent to risk management.

Self-Insurance Institute of America
P.O. Box 15466
Santa Ana, CA 92735
(714) 508-4920

Actuaries, attorneys, claims adjusters, consultants, insurance companies, corporations, risk managers, and third party administrators are the backbone of this organization. The institute promotes alternative methods of risk protection as opposed to conventional insurance—that is, promoting the transfer of risk from an insurance company to the individual employer. The Self-Insurance Institute of America seeks to improve the quality of self-insurance plans, while protecting the industry from adverse legislation and regulations. The association also provides educational programs for certification and maintains a speakers bureau to provide information on a number of topics, such as economic conditions, human resources, workers' compensation, and so forth.

Shipowners Claims Bureau
    Five Hanover Square
    New York, NY 10004
    (212) 269-2350

This association caters to protection and indemnity insurance management and claims advisors.

Society of Actuaries
    475 North Martingale Road
    Schaumburg, IL 60173-2226
    (847) 706-3500

Founded in 1949 this organization sponsors a series of examinations leading to a member's designation as a Fellow or Associate in the society. The society also maintains a vast library on insurance topics.

Society for Risk Analysis
    1313 Dolly Madison Boulevard
    McLean, VA 22101
    (703) 790-1745

This association of risk assessment professionals promotes the scientific study of risks posed by technological advancement and serves to collect and disseminate information gathered on risk and risk possibilities.

Society of Chartered Property and Casualty Underwriters
   Kahler Hall
   720 Providence Road
   Malvern, PA 19355
   (610) 644-2100

Founded in 1944, this professional society is for individuals who have passed ten three-hour examinations by the American Institute for Property and Liability Underwriters and have been awarded CPCU certification. The society promotes education and research in the field of underwriting and sponsors educational seminars, forums, workshops, and research programs.

Surety Association of America
   1101 Connecticut Avenue NW
   Washington, DC 20036
   (202) 463-0600

Founded in 1908, this association of insurance companies engaged in fidelity, surety, and forgery bond underwriting classifies risks, minimum premiums, and rates. The association also prepares forms, provisions, and riders, and prepares statistical data, acting as an information clearinghouse for members.

United Specialty Agents Alliance
  c/o Statewide Insurance Corporation
  Box 30527
  Phoenix, AZ 85046
  (602) 494-6900

This association of insurance managing general agents creates marketing and advertising campaigns to promote premium production.

Water Quality Insurance Syndicate
  14 Wall Street
  New York, NY 10005
  (212) 292-8100

This confederation of more than fifteen companies insures vessel owners and operators against pollution liability.

Women Life Underwriters Confederation
  5008-45 Pine Creek Drive
  Westerville, OH 43081
  (614) 882-6934

This association of life and health underwriters seeks to advance the life insurance field and informs women members of opportunities in the profession. The association also sponsors educational programs and conducts seminars for members. In addition, the association maintains a speakers bureau.

CHAPTER 7

RELATED CAREERS

In addition to the careers listed earlier in this book, a number of careers in related fields apply to the insurance field as well. In such a case, separate fields overlap, giving insurance practitioners the chance and challenge to work with individuals who have quite different work experiences. The insurance industry has need for such individuals and professions, even though such professions don't necessarily directly relate to the world of insurance. In essence, these ancillary professions can be called support professions, and the practitioners of these fields can be called support personnel. Without them, the world of insurance would run quite a bit less smoothly.

Following are brief descriptions of such professions. Anyone who is interested in working within the insurance field in a capacity other than as an insurance practitioner is urged to research the various avenues available in pursuing career paths in these professions.

ATTORNEYS

Because of the complexity of insurance policies and state regulations, insurance providers often employ attorneys to assist them in proper procedures and the methods of instituting legally sound insurance practices.

Attorneys serve as both advocates and advisors. As advocates, attorneys represent parties in civil cases, such as liability lawsuits, presenting legal arguments in defense of their client (the insurance provider or the insurance policyholder).

As advisors, attorneys counsel insurance providers as to their legal rights and obligations. They also recommend particular courses of action in business.

ACCOUNTANTS

Accountants prepare, analyze, and verify financial reports for insurance providers, guiding these providers toward a financially strong business. Insurance providers may have accountants on staff, or they may hire outside consultants to help them with the recordkeeping of their transactions.

Accountancy personnel also help to maintain accounts payable and accounts receivable departments within insurance agencies and companies. These departments provide up-to-date information regarding transactions between policyholders and the insurance provider. Individual accountants coordinate premium billings, as well as act as liaisons between insurance providers and policyholders in matters related to premiums. In addition, they maintain ledger accounts that pertain to premiums.

HUMAN RESOURCES PERSONNEL

Within an insurance company or agency, there is a need to maintain personnel—coordinating the hiring and replacement of personnel. Often, this task is delegated to human resources personnel. Their duties include the recruitment of new personnel, the administration of employee benefits programs, the administration of wage and salary programs, the administration of payroll programs, the implementation of employee training programs, and the orientation of new employees.

PUBLIC RELATIONS STAFF

Insurance providers rely on public relations practitioners to maintain a strong image of their business while educating the public as to certain programs or benefits. These practitioners, who are communications specialists, prepare brochures and pamphlets regarding the provider, design presentations, develop newsletters, create speeches for management personnel, and write and place news releases with the media. They may also develop web pages, audiovisual presentations, and e-mail communications. By doing this, the public relations practitioner informs the public of insurance opportunities, creating a sense of awareness about the industry.

NURSING AND HEALTH PERSONNEL

Insurance companies and agencies often utilize nursing personnel to maintain medical hot lines, which policyholders contact when in need of referrals for second opinions. These hot lines are also used, in some cases, for the implementation of managed care programs. When employee benefits programs use managed care, employees call these hot lines prior to being admitted to the hospital or another health care provider in order to determine the extent of insurance coverage. Then the consumer can make educated decisions with her or his family physician regarding a hospital stay. In some cases, the hot lines save the consumer from unnecessary medical treatment through an assessment of the consumer's health and a referral for a second medical opinion.

GLOSSARY OF INSURANCE TERMS

Actual cash value   The amount of money a policyholder can expect to recover under the terms of most property insurance policies for damage to or destruction of property. This is subject to the maximum limit of insurance stated in the contract and all other restrictions or requirements within the contract. This amount is what it would take to replace the property at the time of loss, *after* making a fair deduction for depreciation due to wear and tear, obsolescence, or for the degree to which the property has lost its usefulness.

Actual total loss   A type of loss used in marine insurance. If a casualty from insured perils has made it impossible for the insured property to reach its destination, an actual total loss has been suffered. For a contrasting term, see **Constructive total loss.**

Actuary   An expert in the field of insurance mathematics and statistics who deals primarily with problems in the science of rate making.

Adhesion, contract of   An insurance contract prepared by one party, without significant negotiation with the second party, which the second party must essentially accept or reject as is. In cases of ambiguity, a court will lean in favor of the party that did not prepare the contract.

Adjuster   A person who investigates and settles claims for losses incurred under property and casualty policies.

Adjustment   Refers to all of the steps involved in an adjuster's work in settling a claim against an insurer, including investigations, the determination of loss amounts, and settlement agreement.

Agency relationship   The relationship that exists between the agent and the agent's principal. An agency relationship should be of the utmost good faith, especially when insurance is involved.

Agent   One who acts for another. In insurance, the term usually refers to a local agent or a general agent. A local agent acts mainly as a sales and service representative for a company. The local agent has somewhat limited authority, even though he or she is an independent contractor. A general agent supervises company operations within a specified area and has broad managerial powers.

Alien company   An insurance company organized outside the United States. See **Domestic company** and **Foreign company** for contrasting terms.

All risk coverage   A type of insurance policy that protects the insured against loss from any and all perils except those that are specifically listed by the contract as excluded.

Application   A printed form, usually in the nature of a statement or questionnaire, that must be completed by the prospective insured to provide the underwriter with sufficient information to decide whether the risk submitted for insurance is acceptable.

Appraisal clause   A provision in property insurance contracts giving the insurance company and the insured the right to demand an appraisal of the damage by an impartial group of experts. This occurs in the event of failure to come to agreement over the amount of damage to property covered by the policy.

Assessment clause   A provision found in the insurance policies of some mutual insurers and reciprocal exchanges stating the amount member policyholders may be called upon to pay if total losses of the company over a given period of time exceed funds available to cover payment. In numerous instances, such assessments are limited by policy terms to one extra annual premium deposit per policyholder.

Assumption of risk   A defense to a charge of negligence, such as an injured person voluntarily and with knowledge deciding to do something that places her or him at risk. It was also one of the common law defenses used by employers before the advent of workers' compensation laws.

Attorney-in-fact   An individual given legal authority to act for another, generally by means of a contract known as a "power of attorney." In insurance, the manager of a reciprocal exchange is an attorney-in-fact, given power to carry on the daily management and other activities of the exchange.

Average   A term used in marine insurance law to mean partial loss. A general average is a partial loss that generally falls on all the interests at risk in a maritime venture. This loss occurs when some of the property at risk is sacrificed to save the remainder. Particular average is a partial loss that falls on one interest because it is not due to the type of sacrifice to which the law of general average applies.

Aviation insurance   Insurance involving activities having to do with aviation, such as coverage of the aircraft and liability for injury and property damage in the air and on the ground.

Binder   A written agreement that is used when a policy cannot be issued immediately. The terms of a binder are generally thought of as the same as the policy that will replace the binder, unless otherwise stated.

Blanket form   A form of contract. It provides coverage for similar types of property located at different locations or may provide coverage for different types of property at the same location. It also provides coverage for all employees or for a class of employees without their being named.

Broad form A form of contract. Generally, it adds additional perils to the standard form of a policy. The perils added may vary, depending on the type of insurance concerned.

Broker A category of salesperson. According to the usual understanding, a broker does not represent a company, but rather represents the client. He or she may write insurance in a number of companies.

Bureau, rating An organization that gathers loss statistics and other pertinent information essential for rate-making purposes. The rating bureau computes and classifies rates from such data for filing with the state insurance authorities on behalf of its subscribers and member companies.

Business interruption The most common type of insurance for consequential or indirect losses from fire. It pays for a loss of business income when a fire destroys the building in which a business is operating.

Cancellation The policy provision that permits the insurance company to terminate coverage before the end of the policy period. Cancellation provisions are always set forth in the policy.

Claim A request for payment due to loss under a policy of insurance covering the type of loss sustained.

Co-insurance The division of the risk between the insurer and the insured.

Commissioner of insurance A state official normally charged with the duties of regulating insurance company activities in the public interest and administering insurance laws.

Comparative negligence Under these laws, the jury or court decides on the comparative degree of negligence involving the plaintiff and defendant and decides damages on that basis.

Condition A future and uncertain event upon whose happening depends the existence of an obligation in a contract.

Consequential damage or loss   Such damage, loss, or injury as does not flow directly and immediately from the act of the party, but only from some of the consequences or results of such act. In an insurance context, a consequential loss is one that results as the consequence of an event that results in a loss.

Consideration   One of the four required elements in the formation of an informal contract. Both parties must give up something of value in order to form the contract.

Constructive total loss   In marine insurance, constructive total loss occurs when it is still possible for the property to reach its destination, but the cost of getting it there would exceed the value of the property. Thus, the insured notifies the insurance underwriter of the decision to abandon all rights to the property.

Contributory negligence   A defense to a charge of negligence. Contributory negligence is conduct by the plaintiff that contributed (as a legal cause) to the harm the plaintiff has suffered; this conduct falls below the standard to which the plaintiff is required to conform for her or his own protection. It was also one of the common law defenses available to employers of injured workers before the advent of workers' compensation laws.

Cooperation clause   Found in liability policies, providing that upon the insurer's request, the insured shall attend hearings and trials and shall assist in affecting settlements, securing and giving evidence, obtaining the attendance of witnesses, and conducting suits.

Declarations   The page inside the cover of many policies, usually typed or machine printed, providing identifying information concerning the insured, the insured property, and applicable coverages.

Deductible   An amount of money that the insured pays and the insurance company does not. Frequently, it is the first part of a claim amount, after which the insurance company begins paying under the claim.

Direct loss Direct damage to an insured property or person as a result of a loss that is insured against.

Direct-writing company A classification of insurance companies according to their marketing approaches. These are companies that sell insurance by means of their own sales force.

Disability benefit A cash sum paid periodically, such as weekly or monthly, on account of the disability of the insured. Such benefits are paid under automobile and other types of insurance, as well as under workers' compensation provisions.

Dividend In a mutual company, unused portions of the premiums paid by policyholders, returned to them periodically as a savings, after all company loss and operating expenses have been met and something has been added to the surplus fund account. In a stock company, a dividend is that portion of income (earnings) in excess of losses and expenses, distributed to stockholders as a return on their invested capital.

Domestic company A classification of insurance companies according to the location of the home office. It is a company organized in the state to which an individual is referring.

Earned premium That portion of any policy premium that would pay the cost of protection provided by the company up to the present moment.

Endorsement A form printed and attached to an insurance policy, usually in order to add something to it, take something from it, or otherwise modify or change the policy.

Exclusions Those provisions of a policy that describe types of property, perils, hazards, or other items for which no coverage is provided.

Experience Generally, the total loss record of a company for a given period or the actual loss record on particular classes of insurance for such a period.

Experience rating   A rating device for comparing the loss record of a particular risk with the average loss record of all other risks of the same general class.

Exposure   A term expressing the fact that something is subject to possible loss from some peril or hazard. For example, a home exposed to gasoline tanks could be said to have a severe exposure to the perils of fire or explosions.

Extended coverage   An endorsement or section of one of the standard insurance forms usually attached to a basic fire insurance policy to extend it for coverage of such perils as windstorms, hail, and explosions.

Federal crime insurance   Insurance provided in order to insure against burglary, robbery, and other theft against property and persons. It was enacted because of the difficulty encountered by property owners in obtaining commercial coverage in areas where the crime rate was expected to be high.

Federal flood insurance   Insurance provided in order to make coverage available in areas that experience a high incidence of flooding and where commercial companies are unable to provide coverage at an affordable premium.

Federal riot insurance   Designed to provide property insurance for areas that are faced with potential riot damage and that cannot purchase coverage from commercial companies.

Fidelity bond   A contract under which any losses sustained by an employer due to the dishonesty of an employee covered by the contract are made good by the insurance company as surety.

Fire-resistive   Referring to a type of property judged by strict engineering standards as having an unusual capacity to resist fire. This term is used in insurance circles as a preference to the more popularly used term "fireproof," because there is not actually a type of property that is not subject to damage by fire.

Floater policy   A form often used synonymously with inland marine policies, but more accurately defined as a policy covering property in the course of transportation, wherever it may be moved. Such policies frequently cover the same property on the premises where it is normally located.

Foreign company   A classification of an insurance company according to the location of the home office. A foreign company is one organized in another state of the United States.

Hazard   A condition of circumstances increasing the likelihood that loss will occur.

Homeowner's policy   A package policy combining property insurance with liability coverage. Coverage is integrated with fixed relationships among the coverages, with a single premium applying to the whole package.

Indemnity   Compensation for damage, loss, or injury incurred. Property and casualty insurance policies are usually contracts of indemnity that reimburse for the amount of loss rather than pay a particular amount without regard for the amount of loss. The latter type of contract is a valued contract.

Inland marine insurance   Insurance provided to take care of property while it is on land during transit. Its major types are transportation policies, bailee insurance, and personal property coverage.

Inspection   A report used in underwriting. Inspection consists of checking public information, such as traffic report records and financial filings, and interviewing persons likely to have pertinent information concerning the proposed insured and her or his business operation.

Insurable risk   A risk that has the characteristics that make it insurable. The characteristics are that it must be susceptible to the law of large numbers, the occurrences of loss must be uncertain, the loss must be of a nature to cause significant difficulty, losses must be irregular in occurrence, the cost of insuring the risk must be low in comparison to the coverage, and the risk must be determinable.

Insurance   A contract by which one party, for a compensation called the premium, assumes particular risks of the other party and promises to pay to her or him, or to her or his nominee, a certain or ascertainable sum of money on a specified contingency.

Insuring clauses   Clauses, usually printed in the policy, that set forth the consideration being provided, the specifics of what is being insured, the promise to pay the amount of damages agreed on, and similar provisions.

Interinsurance company   Also called the reciprocal; a system under which several individuals may underwrite each other's risks against various hazards through an attorney-in-fact common to all, under an agreement that each underwriter acts separately for one another.

Lapse   A situation in which an insurance policy has automatically ceased to remain in force beyond a specified date because of the policyholder's failure to pay a premium.

Liability insurance   Insurance providing protection for a person's legal responsibility for acts that result in injuries to other persons or damages to other persons' property.

Licensing   The procedure for applying for, qualifying for, and issuing a license to carry on an insurance activity.

Limit of liability   The maximum amount the insurance company is obligated to pay under the coverage. Generally, liability limits are different for different coverage within one policy.

Lloyd's organization   A type of insurer, the best known being Lloyd's of London. Each member of Lloyd's is an individual insurer.

Loss ratio   The proportion of the premiums received by the insurer that are paid out in losses. If more is paid out than is taken in, rates are not adequate.

Malpractice insurance   A type of liability insurance that insures against legal liability on account of improper or negligent treatment or procedures by the insured or a person under the direction of the insured.

Manual rating   The most common type of rating done. Risks that are similar are charged a rate contained in the manual of rates, since they are likely to produce similar loss results.

McCarran-Ferguson Act (Public Law 15)   The federal law that states that the regulation of the business of insurance shall remain a matter of state control except in those areas where Congress has declared otherwise with specific legislation.

Misrepresentation   A deliberate misstatement of a material fact about the proposed subject matter of insurance, fraudulently made by an applicant to persuade the underwriter to cover a risk that the underwriter would not have covered if he or she had known the facts.

Named peril policy   The type of policy that lists the particular perils that are covered. Any unnamed perils are excluded or not covered.

National Association of Insurance Commissioners (NAIC)   The association of state insurance department heads. The organization meets to exchange ideas, discuss matters of mutual interest, and formulate model legislative bills having to do with insurance.

Negligence   The omission of something that a reasonable person, guided by those ordinary considerations that regulate human affairs, would do or the doing of something that a reasonable and prudent person would not do.

No-fault automobile insurance   An approach to automobile insurance where everyone who is injured, either bodily or by damage to property, can first recover from her or his own insurance company without resorting to legal action. More serious or costly damages can be recovered through legal action.

Non-participating insurance   Insurance issued by stock companies that are said not to participate in the earnings of the company, since no policy dividends are payable from the company's surplus.

Notice of loss   The provision in a policy calling for the notification of the insurer and a later filing of appropriate proof in the event of a loss covered by the policy.

Obligee   A term used with bonds. It is the person to whom the surety's promise is made on behalf of the principal.

Ocean marine insurance   Types of insurance involving transportation of goods over oceans and similar bodies of water.

Partial disability   A term used in workers' compensation. Partial disability impairs earning ability but does not involve a total inability to work. It may be required that partial disability follow a period of total disability in order that compensation be payable.

Participating insurance   Insurance issued by mutual companies and, in some instances, by stock companies that participate in the earnings of the company in that dividends are payable to the policyholder from the surplus of the company.

Paul v. Virginia   The case, decided by the United States Supreme Court in 1868, that held that the business of insurance was not commerce.

Peril   The risk, hazard, or contingency insured against by a policy of insurance. Peril also states the possible cause of loss. Fire and hail are perils, for example.

Premium   The payment, or one of the periodic payments, a policyholder agrees to make for an insurance policy.

Principal   A term used with bonds. The surety agrees to compensate the obligee, on behalf of the principal, if the principal does not perform as agreed. The principal is the one who is to do the performing.

Proof of loss   Part of the provisions in the policy having to do with notice of loss and providing information. The proof is the evidence as to the loss itself.

Protection   In general, the total coverage provided by an insurance policy.

Proximate cause   That which, in a natural and continuous sequence, produces injury and without which the resultant injury would not have occurred.

Rate-making   The process of establishing a rate that is correct for the risk. Principles involved are non-discrimination, rate adequacy, economic practicality, rate moderateness, and non-fluctuation in rates.

Real property   Land or real estate. Other property is personal property. Generally, real property includes the buildings located on it and fixtures affixed to the buildings.

Reasonable person   The fictitious person who serves as the standard for deciding whether the defendant has acted in a negligent fashion.

Representation   An oral or written statement by the insured to the insurer, made prior to the completion of the contract, giving information as to some fact with respect to the subject of the insurance.

Reserve   The measure of the funds that an insurance company holds specifically for fulfillment of its policy obligations. Methods of calculating reserves are prescribed by law.

Retrospective rating   A type of rate-making based on the insured's own loss experience, where the insured and insurer negotiate a minimum and maximum premium for the year. The premium eventually paid, usually between the maximum and minimum, is based on experience.

Risk   The danger or hazard of loss of the insured's property. Generally, risk is indicated and calculated as a percentage, with the percentage having to do with the probability of loss.

Safe driving plan   Private passenger automobile insurance rates are based on the individual's driving record and those of other drivers who reside with the insured. Not only are convictions for traffic offenses taken into account, but also accidents where the insured or another driver was not at fault.

Salvage   A term used with bonds. It is the amount recovered from the employee who is the subject of a fidelity bond. The contract determines which party of the contract will receive the salvage.

Schedule form   A policy form that lists separate items at several locations. Each item of personal property or building is specifically described, but all are covered by the same form, with the amount of coverage on each item being the proportionate share of the total amount of all items.

Schedule rating   A type of rating applicable when the insured has undertaken loss prevention techniques. The insured provides a schedule indicating loss prevention measures; these products rate deviations.

Self-insurance   When self-funding an insurance plan, an employer assumes the risk normally passed on to the insurance company. This is done in an effort to control costs, save money, and gain internal control of an insurance plan.

Southeastern Underwriters v. United States   The case, decided by the United States Supreme Court in 1944, that held that the business of insurance is interstate commerce.

Standard fire insurance policy   The commonly used and standardized policy used for fire insurance coverage on buildings. It is frequently enhanced by extended coverage.

Stock company   A classification of insurance companies by the way they are organized. A stock company is one in which an initial capital investment is made by the subscribers to the stock, and the business is thereafter conducted by a board of directors elected by the stockholders. The distribution of earnings or profits is determined by the board of directors.

Strict liability   Liability without the necessity of establishing that the defendant is at fault. It is generally found in cases where dangerous materials are in use.

Subsequent injury   A term used with workers' compensation. It is an injury sustained by an employee who has suffered a previous injury, such that the disability resulting from the combined effect of the two injuries is greater than would have been due to the second injury alone.

Superseded suretyship   A rider attached to a fidelity bond that provides that any loss occurring under the prior bond, which would have been paid if that bond had continued in force, will be paid by the new bond.

Surety   A term used with bonds. Surety is the person (frequently with an insurance company) who makes good the promise of the principal to the obligee.

Surety bond   A contract under which a person (surety) agrees to perform on behalf of the principal that which has been promised the obligee. It covers the financial strength of the covered person, the person's honesty, her or his ability, or a combination of these.

Tenants' form   A form of the homeowners' policy applicable to those who rent the dwelling. Essentially all of the coverages of the homeowners' package are included in this form, except those applying to the dwelling.

Term insurance   A life insurance policy that is to remain in force over a relatively short period for the purpose of protecting the beneficiary named against premature death of the insured.

Theft insurance   Coverage against various forms of theft. Many theft policies pertain to only some of the forms of theft, while others pertain to nearly all forms.

Time limits provisions   Provisions in policies that impose limitations as to when claims must be submitted and proofs of loss submitted, how soon lawsuits may be started, and how long after a loss a suit may be brought.

Tort   Any wrongful act, damage, or injury done willfully, negligently, or in circumstances involving strict liability, but not involving breach of contract, for which a civil suit can be brought.

Transportation insurance   Coverage for instrumentalities of transportation and the goods being transported. It is a type of inland marine insurance. Policies cover either the property itself or the acts of the insured, the insured's employee, or the insured's agent.

Unearned premium   The part of the original premium charged for the insurance that cannot be considered "earned" by the company beyond the current date, since protection still must be provided throughout the remaining life of the contract.

Uninsured motorists' insurance   Insurance that provides for payment to the insured for damages to which he or she is entitled because of bodily injury, sickness, or disease caused by the owner or operator of an uninsured automobile.

Valued contract   A type of insurance contract. It pays the insured or the insured's beneficiary a certain amount or value regardless of the loss incurred.

Vicarious liability laws   These laws hold the owner of a car or other vehicle responsible for liability arising from the use of the vehicle by another person so long as the person using it is driving with the permission of the owner.

Waiting period   A term used with disability income as provided under workers' compensation, automobile insurance, and health insurance. It is the period that must elapse, following the onset of disability, before payments under the policy begin.

Waiver   A voluntary and intentional relinquishment of a known and existing right. The term is applied when a party, usually by its conduct, acts in such a way as to abandon a requirement that would otherwise be necessary.

Warranty   A statement on the part of the insurer, frequently appearing in the policy or in another instrument incorporated into the policy, relating to the risk insured against. A warranty is a part of the contract.

Workers' compensation   Statutes that brought forth the idea of strict liability on the part of employers for the injuries of employees while they were at work. The costs of compensation are considered legitimate costs of production, which should be shifted to the consumer as part of the cost of the goods produced.

APPENDIX B

RELATED READING

Following is a list of publications about the insurance industry. Persons interested in the insurance business may want to use them as additional sources of reference.

Alterman, Edward and Irwin Vanderhood. *The Strategic Dynamics of the Insurance Industry.* New York: McGraw-Hill, 1996.

Baldwin, Ben G. *The Complete Book of Insurance* New York: McGraw-Hill, 1997.

Kenney, Roger. *Insurance Industry.* Schaumburg, IL: Alliance of American Insurers, 1977.

Prichard, Julia and Louis Jordan. *Managing Change in the Insurance Industry.* New York: American Educational Systems, 1999.

Rudman, Jack. *Insurance Agent—Insurance Broker.* Syosset, NY: National Learning Corporation, 1994.

Sundheim, Finn A. *How to Insure a Business.* Santa Barbara, CA: Venture Publications, 1995.

Williams, Arthur, Michael Smith, and Peter Young. *Risk Management and Insurance.* New York: McGraw-Hill, 1997.